Destination Life

Destination Life

Journey to a Life of Prosperity, Fulfillment, and Abundant Blessings

SANDRA RHODES

iUniverse, Inc.
New York   Bloomington

Destination Life
Journey to a Life of Prosperity, Fulfillment, and Abundant Blessings

iUniverse books may be ordered through booksellers or by contacting:

iUniverse
1663 Liberty Drive
Bloomington, IN 47403
www.iuniverse.com
1-800-Authors (1-800-288-4677)

ISBN: 978-1-4401-7058-4 (pbk)
ISBN: 978-1-4401-7060-7 (cloth)
ISBN: 978-1-4401-7059-1 (ebk)

Library of Congress Control Number: 2009910173

Printed in the United States of America

iUniverse rev. date: 12/1/2009

In loving memory of my husband
Ronald Eugene Rhodes
August 14, 1951- March 15, 2008
The one I laughed with, the one I dreamed with
The one who made my life complete
You are forever loved

To my children, whom I have been so blessed to have in my life; no words can express the love that I have for you. Tyrah, Tommy, Sarah, Michael, Nathan and Samantha.

To my beautiful grandchildren; you have tripled my blessings and have multiplied the love in my life a million times over. Elijah, Elisha, Brenden and Makaila.

To my niece, Melissa, I love you so much, and to her wonderful husband Rich. You have both been so much help with this book. Thank you.

Contents

PART THREE *It's All About Family*

PART FOUR *Making It Work*

PART FIVE *Live, Learn, Grow*

Destination Life

Introduction

This is not just another book you are going to read through once and then pass on to a friend or family member. This is a book you are going to want to keep close by for a long time. You will scribble it up with reminders, use highlighters in a variety of colors, ear mark pages, and carry it around with you until the cover falls off. If this book becomes a part of your life then I have accomplished my goal.

Destination Life is filled with all of the wisdom you are going to need to pick yourself up, no matter where you are at right now, and plop yourself onto the road of life where you will drive to your most desired destinations. Remember, it is not arriving that is the most rewarding and exciting part of a journey, but the journey itself. On this journey you are going to truly become more prosperous, fulfilled, and blessed beyond what you ever dreamed possible.

You are going to make a lot of stops and visit thrilling places that are going to fill you with an electrifying wonder of life. You are going to open yourself to all of the exciting possibilities that await an eager and motivated traveler.

This is your journey and no one's journey through this life will ever be the same. You will, maybe for the first time in your life, realize how blessed you are with both material and non material treasures, and you are going to learn how to achieve even more.

On this journey, you will begin to see beyond unpaid bills, unfulfilled dreams, heartaches and hardships. You will drive your car, which represents your life, toward your future of prosperity, blessings, dreams you once thought unreachable, and a real sense of inner peace and happiness.

As you read, you will begin to put everything you have learned to use right away, because everything in *Destination Life* is easy to use, understand, and remember. You won't need to bring anything along with you except your own motivation and positive energy. *The time to begin your journey is right now!*

You are going to witness a transformation in your life. You are beginning a thrilling journey that is going to take you places you have never been before, and back to places you have been, but with new meaning and understanding.

You will learn how to use the simple tools of life, that you already possess, that will propel you toward the life you have dreamed about. You will learn how to set goals and then how to move toward those goals, taking tiny steps if necessary, until you have achieved one goal after another.

Your dreams are central to your success. Your dreams are the gas in your car, constantly moving you forward. So, dream big and fill your tank to the fullest.

On your journey you will learn secrets. Secrets that are so simple that you are going to wonder how you missed them. These secrets will enrich your life and add to your already abundant blessings. These are secrets that have always existed, but in your hurry to get through life, and with all your daily challenges, you have missed them. These secrets are going to enrich your life, expand your knowledge, and give your very existence new meaning.

You will, on this journey, tap into your faith. Faith will free you of needless worry, anxiety, and stress. Your time is too valuable to waste on these useless emotions. With faith you will learn to live your life to the fullest, grasping everything life has to offer. You will no longer fear the thrill of taking risks, but will embrace its thrilling powers.

Most important, you will learn about empathy, sharing, and helping your fellow traveler. You will realize that just as vessels of hope sail through your life when you need them, that you also will be the vessel of hope through the life of another. The power of understanding, and your willingness to help others, will reward you beyond your wildest dreams.

The journey you are about to take is not one in which you will passively sit and watch the scenery pass; you are going to be an active participant.

As your journey unfolds you will feel confused and unsure. Start right now by tossing all of those negative feelings right out the window. You are embarking on a wondrous and exciting journey that will overflow with adventure as well as challenges.

You are a powerful traveler. Buckle up your seat belt, hold on, and get ready to take off on a wonderful adventure through life.

Part One

Road To Success

✦

Chapter 1
Tools Of Success: The Beginning

✦

The very soul of *Destination Life* is learning to understand and use the power of *faith, patience,* and *perseverance.* The power of this trio will penetrate, transform, and move your life toward your dreams and goals. This unbendable foundation will become your strength and shield, as you empower yourself with a force you may have never thought possible.

As you begin to apply faith, patience, and perseverance to your life, you will not only see changes, but you will live these changes. You are going to change how you look at life, and in doing so, your life is going to change. So, let's delve right into the transforming powers of *Destination Life.*

Your life is overwhelming. Imagine this scenario. You've had a lousy day at work. You crawl home through bumper-to-bumper traffic. When you arrive home your house is in a shambles. You'd think that since you get home every single day, at exactly the same time that the house would be clean; but no, the house is torn up. The kids are screaming at each other. The babysitter left (hours ago.) You forgot she told you she had to pick her nephew up at the airport. At any rate, the kids are home alone. The dog pound left a leash law notice at your door informing you that your beloved pet (the one you had before the kids) is at the pound. The laundry is stacked to the ceiling, even though you just did five loads the day before. You forgot to thaw something out for dinner, and tonight they really want to eat something healthy and not their usual diet of cereal and pizza. The microwave just saw its last frozen burrito. Your ex just called to inform you that he knows the kid's were home alone and he doesn't approve. Baths and homework loom in the very near future and quite frankly you just don't give a damn. Overwhelming? I think so. Sadly, this scenario is a simple one compared to thousands of others.

This is an example of one of the many times you will rely on your faith, patience, and perseverance. So, let's see how this trio can work for you. First, you'll blow it (and it will be well deserved, even if no one else thinks so.) Next, you'll say hateful things that will leave you feeling guilty for weeks (and I guarantee you that they won't forget the exact words you used.) Last, you'll slip into a deep and lonely black hole of depression (but no one will notice.) After you take these progressive and predictable steps, you'll return to the problem. The scenario doesn't matter, ultimately, you'll come back to the problem, which isn't the house, or the kids, or your ex-spouse. The problem is your unique situation and what you are going to do about it.

Stop! **RIGHT NOW,** and focus on the situation you're in. Become aware of the strength that is flowing through you. The key words here are, *stop* and *focus*. Not on the house, or the dog, or the kids screaming in the background. Go somewhere where you can focus. Slip into the bathtub, sit in your car, lock yourself in your room, or just sit down in the middle of the chaos (some people think better when it's noisy and chaotic.)

When you get to where you want to be and are comfortable, whisper these words: "faith, patience, perseverance, faith, patience, perseverance." Become aware of how much faith, patience, and perseverance are already a part of your life. Know that these three tools have the power to transform your life as you learn to use them and allow their power to work its magic. I promise that before you finish reading this book, these principles will be woven into the very fabric of your soul.

There are three working components to the principles of faith, patience, and perseverance. They are: *do it, deal with it,* and *this to will pass.* Sound too easy? It is easy, so there will be no excuses for you not to succeed. Living the life you were meant to live, completely happy and fulfilled, is a full time job. Your only limit on this perfectly fulfilled life is time. The short time you have in this life should motivate you into achieving and living your dreams; meaning, **RIGHT NOW!** You have no time to waste in this life, there is just too much to do, and see, and become.

Let's begin by looking at these six power tools and learn how they work together to make you a whole and self-fulfilled person. It is very important that you feel special and fulfilled as a person. You've heard the cliché: there is only one you in this world. Well, I'm going to take that cliché a little further and tell you that not only are you the only *you* in this world, but you are filled with power. This power can take you anywhere you want to go and allow you to be anyone or anything you want to be. At the very least it will allow you to accept your limitations, what ever they may be, and allow you to live happily within those limits.

Unhappiness and failure are not a part of your journey, no matter what your situation. You are going to learn how you can start applying the laws of faith, patience, and perseverance to your life right now. Starting this minute, you are going to take control of your life and of your emotions. You are going to be the captain of your ship! Isn't it exciting to know that you are about to embark on a journey where you and those you love and care about will all come out winners? There are no other options; you are a winner, you are blessed, you are filled with power. This is your journey, enjoy it.

Chapter 2

Faith: The Power

✦

What exactly is faith? Faith believes the unbelievable without having to see, smell, touch, or feel it. You are never alone with faith. Faith replaces worry. Faith is making a choice, then waiting for the results and the consequences of that choice; then molding the outcome into something positive for you. Faith is never being sorry for the outcome of your choices.

When things are going wrong it is likely that you are not doing what you should have been doing in the first place. In other words, bad things force you to reevaluate your situation. When things are going good, leave it alone. Faith gives you the freedom and the desire to evaluate your life for possible change.

Worry produces no results. Faith is your friend, counselor, parent, and companion. There are no wrong choices with faith, only wrong turns that can be quickly changed, without the burden of guilt. When faith becomes a part of your life, fear and worry become obsolete.

Faith will not make you super human, only super alert. You will rely on someone or something greater than yourself, no matter what that force may be for you. Not a day passes that I don't ask for the faith to have faith. Who do I ask? I ask whatever power I want to ask, be it nature, the air, or God. Simply stated; faith is the acceptance of all choices you make, and going with the flow of your life. Faith is not questioning life, but living life to the fullest. Faith is forging past the painful times and learning to accept that even turbulent times have a place in your life. How you react to life's challenges is what is important. Imagine all the extra time you are going to have after tossing those useless energy zappers worry, guilt, and fear out of your life.

It takes time for real faith to become a part of your life. You'll know when you have achieved true faith; you'll feel it. Compare faith to living at home with your parents. At home you are a member of a team (the family.) You tell your parents what you want and then your parents make the final choices. You accept the choices they make and know everything will work out for the best, because you trust them. Faith is your parents making the final choices for you. Go with it and trust in your faith. There will be times when you aren't sure what you want, but things always somehow work out; this is faith in action. Wait for the final result, sometimes it comes as a surprise. You've met people who shrug and say, "I don't know how it happened." Or others who say, "If this didn't happen I wouldn't be here now." This, my friend, is faith in action. Faith does not wait, faith happens.

Let me tell you a story I heard a long time ago and it really is the essence of faith: There was once a great storm and a man moved up to the second floor to stay dry. A boat came past and the man on the boat called to the man, "come into my boat and I will save you."

"No," the man replied. "I have faith, God will save me," The storm grew worse and the water rose higher. Another boat approached.

"Jump into my boat, I will save you."

"No," the man replied, "I have faith, God will save me," and he moved further up to the roof.

A third boat came past. "Quickly, jump, I will save you," the third man called.

"No," the man replied, trusting in his faith.

Then the man found himself in heaven standing before God. "What happened?" he asked. "I had faith, I trusted in you, what happened?"

God looked sadly at the man and replied. "I sent help three times, my son.

Faith is going with the flow and accepting help when it is sent to you. You must open yourself and know when help has arrived. Keep your faith. Help sometimes comes in surprising ways. What you need isn't always going to be something you are familiar with. Your needs and prayers are answered in many different ways. It is your job to open your eyes to all of the possibilities that may be answers you are seeking. Open your mind and be aware that what you are looking for won't come in just black and white; there are going to be vast shades of gray.

Mastering the art of faith isn't easy. No matter how uncomfortable or unhappy worry makes us, most of us thrive on it. Worry is a very important part of our lives, but it doesn't have to be. Now is the time to release your stress, worry, and fear, and replace it with faith.

Money problems, kids running wild, relationship issues, Housing, family, loss, loneliness, these are all issues that are covered under faith. No matter how bad your situation may be, faith has the power to propel you forward. And ultimately, that's what it's all about, moving forward.

You are not superhuman. Give faith time to grow and become a part of you. You are going to use the principles of patience and perseverance to build on your faith. Remember faith, patience, and perseverance are a trio.

To begin, you must learn new ways of thinking, and you will. You must learn new ways of planning and living your life. Most important, you must learn new ways of feeling, especially when you blow it, and you will. It isn't going to be long before faith becomes a part of your life and you feel the difference.

Your life is cluttered with thousands of responsibilities. Thank God, you have the opportunity to eliminate the wasteful acts of stress, worry, and fear, and begin to live your life in faith.

Chapter 3

Perseverance: The Strength

✦

Keep achieving, keep moving, and keep believing. Your eyes and heart must always face in the direction you want your life to move. Keep in mind that the direction you want your life to be facing today may change tomorrow, for what ever reason, and that's okay. It's okay to put your goals on hold, but it's not okay to throw them away. Holding on to your goals and dreams no matter where they seem to be going (or not going) is the essence of perseverance.

"Throw away my goals," you say, "why would I do that?" There are hundreds of reasons and excuses why people forget about their goals or just toss them out the window. Maybe you've had a tragedy in the family. Maybe financially you're barely making it or you've suffered a major set back such as a job loss. These are the times when your faith will be tested, when you will discover how faith and perseverance work together to benefit you.

To truly understand perseverance you have to have faith. Faith opens your mind to the knowledge and belief that everything has a purpose and that purpose is working in your life, even in the worst of times.

No matter what you chose to do in this life there will be obstacles. There will be excuses for failure, reasons for why you can't achieve your goals, and arguments for staying safely on the bottom.

Let's pretend that one of your dreams is to return to school; maybe you have always wanted to get a degree in law. Let's explore some reasons why that could never be a possibility for you. You're too old, you can't afford a babysitter, you're too tired after a long day at work, you don't spend enough time with the family, or you're just too busy. Okay, okay, these are all good and valid reasons, **if you allow them to be.**

Now here's where your faith kicks in. Start by talking to a more powerful source. This source could be a moment of prayer, a moment of silence, or just time to allow your mind to clear itself of clutter. What ever that higher source is for you, let it kick in and take over your thoughts for a moment. Give yourself a good, long, and introspective pep talk. Explore all of the reasons why you can't go back to school, then tell yourself why you **can** go back to school. For the next few days let these thoughts gently flow through your mind; not consuming your thoughts every minute, but gently flowing like a soft wind blowing over a lake, until magically, before you realize it, a plan will materialize and as always things will fall into place.

Of course there will be steps you will have to take; faith and goals must have action to propel them. While you are waiting for a final answer to materialize, and while you are waiting for your goals to take shape, you can begin to take tiny baby steps. Maybe you could sign up for one class a week. This may seem like a waste of time, but you are moving toward your goal. Nothing is ever lost if you are even one step closer to where you want to be.

Never stop believing in and working toward your goals and dreams. Goals and dreams are the substance of your life. Life is fun, exciting, challenging, and mysterious. Take everything you are entitled to from it. Think of life as a season pass; some people pay for season passes and never use them, while others get every penny out of them. *You must persevere*! Don't allow that season pass to just sit, **USE IT!**

The fabric of your life is your dreams and goals. Maybe you want to conquer a drug or alcohol problem, begin a new career, travel, or just boost your income. There is no such thing as a silly or useless dream or goal. There is no goal that is a waste of time. You will have and achieve many goals and dreams in your life. Some goals and dreams come to you in ways you would never expect, materializing from seemingly nowhere. Open your mind to all you have already achieved and to everything that has already fallen into your life.

Goals and dreams all serve a purpose in life. All of our successful goals and dreams, and all the ones we continue to strive toward, all have a place in our lives and make up who we are. Goals and dreams tell our story. The best part of goals and dreams is planning and anticipating just like you did as a child during the Christmas season. Everything is within your grasp; half the fun is getting there. Goals, dreams, and the fulfillment of them become your story. Never stop wanting, planning, and achieving.

Faith is your guide; have faith and persevere. All that you are dreaming of and working toward will come. Keep your eyes and mind open, the end results of your dreams and labors may not come in the form you envision. Don't walk away from what you worked to achieve because it didn't come in the form you expected.

To persevere is to hold in there no matter what, no matter how hard or hopeless things may seem or actually be. Every desire you have is around the corner. Want it? Go for it, have faith, and persevere. Every dream, when the season is right, will be harvested. Faith and perseverance go hand-in-hand; use them to your advantage. When you succeed, those around you reap the rewards, be it your spouse, your children, or your friends. Everyone wins when you persevere.

Chapter 4

Patience: The Test

✦

Patience is the third of this powerful trio, but certainly not the least important. The word is self explanatory. If you have relied on your faith and you have persevered, then it only stands to reason you will now have to tap into your patience. All of your desires and needs will come. There is no set time when success will knock on your door, but it will. Don't be fooled when your dreams and goals come in a different form then you had planned; look for possibilities in every success story. Be patient. Remember, the harvest must be ripe.

Let's use a pregnant woman as our example. A pregnant woman is excited, full of joy and anticipation about the new life growing within her. She is full of dreams for the child she will soon welcome into her life. A good portion of her day is filled with all of the wonderful things she will do with the baby when he or she is born. It takes Nine months for this miracle to happen, patience, patience, patience. When the time is right, the mother will be blessed with a perfect and beautiful child, but only when the time is right. Only when the harvest is ripe will things happen and our perseverance and patience will pay off. We all know that it would be a disaster for a child to be born too early, and so it is with our dreams and goals, the time must be right, the harvest must be ripe.

Patience goes hand-in-hand with faith and perseverance. Use it and everything you could possibly need or want will come in its own good time. Have faith, persevere, and have patience. Sometimes you won't get what you asked for or wanted, but something just as good or better will take its place, something you never expected. Have patience.

Here's a little song I used to sing to my children when they were growing up. As they grew older they sang along with me and now the oldest of the bunch sing it to their own children.

Have patience, have patience, don't be in such a hurry. When you rush, when you rush, it only makes you worry. Remember, remember, that God is patient too. Think of all the times when others had to wait on you.

Time is a valuable commodity. Don't fill this limited treasure with unnecessary worry and stress. Have patience and enjoy your limited gift of time, while outside forces take care of the things you need. Life is a series of circles, with little circles within the big one.

> ➤ *Make a choice*
> ➤ *Set a goal*
> ➤ *Take steps*
> ➤ *Have faith*
> ➤ *Persevere*
> ➤ *Have patience*

The circle is now complete.

Chapter 5

Do It: The Action

✦

There are three actions you will use with your faith, patience, and perseverance. One of the worst habits you can get into is the habit of procrastination; we all do it. It's going to take a lot of motivation and self discipline to stop this nasty and self defeating habit.

Self discipline and a desire to see a change in your life is all the motivation you are going to need. Start with small steps to break the habit of procrastination. You know that dress you bought that was too small, the one that's been sitting in your closet for weeks? Well, get it out of your closet and return it to the store. Returning the dress will be both a hassle and good practice for you. But there is an added benefit. You can pick up a cuter dress or have a little extra cash in your pocket. Breaking the nasty habit of procrastination is the first step in understanding the meaning of; DO IT.

Do it, has two meanings. One of course deals with the idle sin of procrastination. If you have things to do, no matter how tedious, just do it. At the end of the day you are going to feel so much better that you got things done. And believe me, you won't feel like doing it tomorrow either. No better time then now.

We all have days we'd much rather sit at home in front of the television set or curled up with a good book; these are the days you really need to push yourself. Your day of rest is well deserved and in time it will come. Yes, time for you is going to be a very important part of this program. You are important. Your needs are important. Everything you need will happen.

Tedious chores like going to the bank, grocery shopping, or doing the laundry are boring, but they still need to get done. When you finally do get to rest, you won't have to think about all the things you still have to do. *Just do it!* Both work and play are an important part of the circle of our lives and of the stories we are writing.

Do it, is very important when you are facing an obstacle in your life. This could be day care problems, relationship problems, financial problems, or even emotional problems. Take a stand on every issue in your life. Plan a course of action, then **do it.** Remember to use your faith. With your choices will come consequences, which remember, can be changed at any time. Choose a path, then deal with the obstacles on your chosen course. Do it and move on, and with faith this is possible.

Do it, when it comes to those goals and dreams that may seem so out of reach, such as returning to school, starting a new job, or writing that novel you have always dreamed about. Challenge yourself and do it. You can only go to one class a week, okay then do it. Can only write half an hour a day, okay, do it. Every dream has its reward. Do it.

Even failures serve a purpose in your life. Not all of your dreams and goals are going to be successful. The outcome or rewards of your labors may not be what you had planned. Sometimes you will be disappointed and other times you will be glad things worked out differently than what you had in mind. Accept the end results of your goals and dreams and make those results work for you. Don't be disappointed, be surprised. Nothing can stop you, except yourself. Not all failures are truly failures just different endings then what you had planned. And even a different ending can be something wonderful or a possibility you never thought about.

The concept of do it is small but can be easily remembered. It is easy to use and apply to your life. When you come to a fork in the road, make a decision, then do it. No matter what the task or goal, no matter how busy or overextended you are, no matter how hopeless things may seem; plan, make a choice, and do it. And, with faith you will

Chapter 6

This Too Will Pass:
The Reality

✦

This too will pass. Now, here's a phrase you will learn to depend on and use on a regular basis. Not a week passes that I don't remind myself of these wise and comforting words.

Life right now may be overwhelming, unhappy, confusing, or in total turmoil. You have tapped into your faith and you are now going with the flow. Great! You're on the right track. This to will pass is merely words that will reinforce your faith. Words that will remind you that yes, there is a light at the end of the tunnel. This too will pass can be used anytime you are feeling lost, defeated, hopeless, alone, or scared. These words can even be used at work, when you wish the day would just hurry up and end.

These words are simple to remember, effective, and easy to use. This too will pass is a reminder to you that life will go on and you will smile again. All things pass and what ever you are facing today will be gone tomorrow.

In this life, it is a fact that you will face hardships. You will have days that will drag on with no end in sight. You will face trials that seem to be more then you can handle. You will climb mountains. This too will pass is a reminder to keep the faith, persevere, and have patience.

The bad times will pass, the pain, the heartache, and the horror. The experience you are suffering can sometimes be used to help someone else or it might be something you can use to change or better your own life. This too will pass is a gentle reminder that your experience will pass and you will be left with a new strength that is now available for you to tap into.

This too will pass, is a reminder that the good times will also pass. Savor every moment and each unique experience that passes through your life. Appreciate every moment spent with your children, your friends, your family, or just time spent alone. File every little bit of these memories into your heart and soul. There will be a time later in life when those wonderful memories will come rushing back to you. Memories are an heirloom to be passed on to your children, your grandchildren, your great-grand children, and beyond. Give them a wonderful book of memories to carry into their own lives. These memories are a painting into their past and a glimpse into their future.

This too will pass, can be used to pull you through the bad or allow you to savor the good. Remember, no matter what obstacle you face, what challenge, what joy, it will all pass.

Chapter 7

Deal With It: The Battle

✦

The last of the three actions is, *deal with it.* It's merely words that are meant to give you strength. You must repeat these words to yourself over and over again, especially in challenging times. Deal with it can be a powerful force when you apply it to your life.

Whatever you are facing, no matter how devastating, heartbreaking, discouraging, or life shattering, you are going to have to deal with it in one way or another. Your faith will be your strength; but in the end, you are the captain.

Dealing with a problem isn't always going to be an aggressive or physical act. You may deal with a situation by merely having faith, saying a prayer, making a small change in your circumstances, or seeking out help from a professional or a friend. How you choose to deal with a life shattering event will ultimately be up to you, but, you will deal with every situation that passes through your life and you will remain in control. Now is the time to look seriously at your faith. You won't have to turn to alcohol, drugs, violence, or depression as a way of dealing with your problems because you are in control. You are in control of your life and of your situation.

People, who refuse to deal with their life problems, are people who have made an unconscious choice to deal with their problems in negative ways, such as drugs or alcohol. They have now created new problems that must be dealt with.

Every life situation, no matter how small or how life-shattering, will have to be dealt with in one way or another. Your options are to take control of the situation and deal with it in a positive way or you can deal with the problem in negative and self-destructive ways. You can choose to give in and not challenge your problems, but you may be forced to deal with new problems that may be even worse. Not taking control of a life situation may leave you immobilized, out-of-control, and defeated. As you confront each life challenge and make positive choices, it will build on your strength and your ability to meet, face, and conquer those challenges. No matter where the problem goes, remember, this too will pass.

Being in control of your life and emotions is important. Being in control gives you a better chance of survival both mentally and physically. The more in control you are, the easier life's challenges will become. You gain control simply by using your faith. Faith is the open door that you can walk through, and know that there is a power in this universe that will connect with your positive energy, replacing doubt, fear, and negative thoughts with an inner strength. It begins by knowing your thoughts, what you believe, what you fear, and what you want out of life.

You are strong, capable, and in control of your life; tell yourself this and believe it. You will experience a whole new sense of security when you know that you are capable of taking care of things and getting things done. You have the power to fill yourself with a sense of security, confidence, and faith.

You have to deal with life, so deal with it on your terms. Don't allow yourself to become so immobilized that you are unable to pursue your dreams or goals. Life will move on, even if it moves on without you. Control the direction your life is moving in, become an active participant. Make choices to deal with life in ways that are best for you and in ways that you are most comfortable with. You have all the say in where your life is going or you can go where life takes you; it's your choice.

In conclusion, you have six tools to work with as you travel through life.

- ➤ *Faith*
- ➤ *Perseverance*
- ➤ *Patience*
- ➤ *This too will pass*
- ➤ *Do it*
- ➤ *Deal with it*

Use these six tools to face life head on. They are simple to use and remember. They can be taken everywhere you go and they will always serve their intended purpose, if you allow them to.

Take control of your life, live your life, and become an active participant in deciding where your life is headed. You have all the tools you need; use them and move forward. This is your life, your story, your time. Life is an adventure to be lived. All the choices you make will make up the fabric of that life and the essence of who you are and what you desire. Your life is a series of choices and the roads that those choices lead you down.

Everyday you will use your faith, perseverance, and patience. Everyday you will become stronger as you apply to your life the concepts of do it, deal with it, and this too will pass. Everyday that you live you are in the process of writing and living a wonderful story, *your story*. Good or bad, your story will be written; make it a wonderful experience. Even the chapters that are filled with sadness and defeat are a part of your story and make you the wonderful person that you are.

Part Two

It's All About Me

✦

Chapter 8

Climbing Mountains

✦

From the day you were born you were faced with mountains and life will continue to put mountains in your path. Life is a series of mountains, some big, some small, and some that seem bigger than they actually are. A toddler learning to walk may, at times, become frustrated and defeated as she struggles to take those first steps. The task of learning to walk to this small child may seem like climbing a mountain, until the inevitable day that she successfully walks.

A child learning to read faces a huge mountain as he struggles through unfamiliar shapes and symbols. Eventually, everything clicks and reading becomes second hand.

Teenagers are faced with huge mountains as their emotions rage out of control. Then, the day arrives when everything falls together for them and the events that were once viewed as mountains become nothing more than experiences that will be filed away in their memories.

So it is with you. As you grow and change you will be faced with mountains; not one but many. As you live life, no matter what stage you are in, life is going to hand you wonderful riches and treasures. It will also give to you challenges, such as the loss of a loved one, job loss, loss of home, loss of a spouse, relationship issues, child rearing problems, family issues, and the list goes on. Dreams and goals aren't going to just happen; they are going to take work. These are your mountains.

Look at each mountain in your life and be prepared to face the challenge of climbing it. Every mountain has to be crossed. You can trail blaze a road around the mountain, you can struggle over it, or you can sit down and refuse to do anything. Life allows you to make all the choices in where and how you want your life to go.

You are given an abundance of tools to face the journey over these mountains. You are blessed with an ability to tap into your motivation, energy, faith, and most important, the ability to make choices that have the power to push you toward your goals of happiness and success. Facing a mountain is a challenge, but crossing the highest of mountains can be a rewarding and successful experience.

If you have a plan, a goal, the motivation to succeed, and faith, you have no choice but to be successful. Your job is to make things happen. Armed with your life tools, you will either climb the mountain or find a way around it.

Maybe you are looking for greater financial security; this is your mountain. Once you have an idea of what you want, it is time to, *plan, set goals*, and *act*. Your plan to change your financial picture may be to go back to school and become a registered nurse. Three or four years down the road, after struggling with children, money, car problems, and relationship issues, you are going to one day be over that mountain and you will have realized a dream, conquered a goal, and succeeded.

There is a way over every mountain. The journey and the obstacles you face will become a part of your story. Refusing to make choices, looking at the mountain and groaning, and manipulating others to go over the mountain for you isn't going to work. You have to cross every mountain yourself. You will find and tap into support systems. Every journey has a special blessing that will inspire, guide, and reward you; be open to these treasures. But ultimately, the journey is yours.

The journey over a mountain isn't always a negative experience. There are some journeys that although challenging, give life meaning for an entire life time. Someone who dedicates their life to helping others, such as Mother Teresa, climbed numerous mountains, but it was her journey and one that gave her life complete meaning.

Families that spend their entire lives raising foster children and even in later years are still raising small children, climb mountains everyday.

The life they have chosen rewards them with all the success they could ever dream of having.

If you have lost a loved one, have lost your health, or some other devastating event has occurred in your life, then the mountain is going to look huge. You may become immobilized, unable to even attempt to climb the mountain. But in your own good time, you will. And at the top you will find the peace and strength you need to finish writing your story and to continue on your journey.

Some experiences in this life are very painful, but you will survive, and will find ways to give your loss meaning. The climb will leave you stronger. You will feel weak for a long time, but once you cross over the mountain, your life will take on a new meaning.

Most of us are in the middle, facing challenges every day. These challenges are our mountains. Getting a new house, getting the kids through college, having or bettering a relationship, starting school, making major life changes, there is no end to the list, and no end to the mountains you might have to climb as your life unwinds; but climb them you will. As you stand before each mountain, before you begin the climb, don't forget to plan, set goals, dream, and have faith.

The good news is that most of the mountains you will climb are really nothing more than mole hills. Every mountain will leave you stronger, wiser, and closer to your goals and dreams.

Chapter 9

Help, My Life Is Out Of Control

✦

Life is not going well. Everything is all wrong. There is nothing good in your life. Financially, you are in a huge slump, the kid's are out of control, you are depressed, lonely, on drugs, losing yourself into a deep and dark pit. How are you going to get back on track? How are you going to take your life back?

There are ways. There are choices. There are new beginnings, but, how will *you* do it? Things are really, really bad, really, really out of control. How are you going to make a change?

Slowly, one step at a time, one day at a time, one hour at a time, even one minute at a time. Today, you are going to start to put yourself back together like a puzzle, one piece at a time. A month might pass and you may have been able to put only one or two pieces of your puzzle together, and that's okay, because you are moving forward and that may be all you can do right now. The most important thing is to start; **start today, right now, this very minute**. As you read these words feel the power creeping over you. Know that you are open to change, you are not afraid. And that, my friend, is the beginning.

Here is a verse from the Bible you might enjoy and take strength from. *The Lord is close to the brokenhearted and saves those who are crushed in spirit. Psalm 34:18.*

The beginning, when you first start to pull your life together, is the most spiritual. You will begin to see, maybe for the first time, an inner self, you may have never known existed. It is the moment you realize you *need* to make a change in your life. It is the moment you realize that you *deserve* more in life than what you now have. It is the moment you realize you *want* a change and are willing to do something to make it happen.

Changes in your life don't have to be drastic; the changes can be gradual, at whatever pace you set for yourself. Start with faith; faith is your most powerful tool. Faith gives you the courage to move forward. In the beginning you will be scared; you will be unsure of what you really want or where you are going, but your faith will carry you through. Faith gives you strength to face the challenges that you will be up against. Nothing worth having is going to be easy to get. You are beginning an uphill climb. Arm yourself with all the tools and resources you will need to conquer and survive. And, *be prepared to succeed!*

Before your journey begins, define the problem or the challenge that you will be up against. What is causing your depression? Your feelings of loss? Your addiction to alcohol or drugs? Your abuse toward your children? The problem has to be defined in order for you to change it. Define the problem; know the battle you are fighting.

At first, your definition of what the problem is may not be completely accurate, and that's okay. As you move forward, you will begin to understand what the real problem is. Define the problem exactly as you see it, right now.

Next, think about all the choices open to you. Think about everything you can do to change your situation. It doesn't matter how silly, impossible, or how crazy your ideas might sound, right now you are only thinking of options and ideas that will propel you forward. For clarity and a quick future reference write your ideas down. Take your time. Sleep on it (for days if you need to) then start to really look at your ideas and pick the one, or several, you think might work for you.

Last, decide on a plan of action and then do it. *Begin.* Take the first step. As you move forward and the issues or problems change, or become clearer, you will have the opportunity to change any or all of your plans. Don't feel that once you decide on a plan of action that you have to follow it, every road has detours and turns. *Don't be afraid to make those turns.* Define what you think the problem is and begin there. Take baby steps. Every step is a move forward no matter how small. Take that step. And have faith.

The steps sound easy, but the actual task will be humongous. You will have to make a commitment to move forward and not give up. Giving up will be easier than plunging forward; but moving forward will have its' rewards. Success is always harder than failure; because you have to work at success. Giving up is always easier than sticking it out; because sticking it out requires a commitment. Burying your head in the sand and pretending life isn't happening is easier than looking life in the face; because looking life in the face and becoming an active participant is a challenge.

> ➤ *Work at life*
> ➤ *Make a commitment*
> ➤ *Become an active participant*
> ➤ *Have faith*
> ➤ *Move forward*

Faith is the beginning. Set a goal with a workable plan, no matter how small, and then have faith that it will happen; because you are going to make it happen. Slowly, you will start to feel the changes that are happening in your life. You will see changes in others who are close to you. Inside, you will feel lighter. What was scary at first will now show itself. You will be turning back onto the road of life. Now, you are ready for bigger steps. It will be scary. It will be a challenge. It will be hard work and at times you will want to crawl back to the place you were at. Remember, failure is easier than success.

Define the problem. Create a plan to change your situation. Set goals. Act. Move forward. It will be that easy and it will be that hard. It will be easy to say and hard to do. It will be easy to want and hard to act. No matter what your goal or plan, it is inevitable that you will have to *do it.* It will be a challenge and a new chapter in your life. You are the writer of your adventure through life and it is up to you to decide how each chapter will play out.

There will be fountains along the way for you to tap into; these fountains will give you strength for the journey. There will be numerous tools that will help and guide you. You may have to join a support group, go to therapy, get a job, read books, or pray. It will be your job to find and use the abundance of tools available to you. Don't miss the fountain; drink when you need to. Take advantage of everything that may move you even one step forward. Keep your eyes open for help you may not realize is here. Everything you need to succeed is right here. It is your job to find what you need and then to have the power and strength to use what you find.

You *can* change the hardships that are handed to you in this life, such as an illness, loss of a loved one, poverty, sadness, or depression. Sometimes we fall victim to our own weaknesses, such as homelessness or drug addiction. No matter how the pain became a part of your life doesn't matter. What matters is facing your challenges. Whatever battle you are fighting will have to be faced and dealt with in some way. Life is a gift, an adventure, and even hardships have their place. To begin to change the hardships in your life is to begin to change how you look at these challenges and obstacles.

Take a deep breath and challenge yourself to move forward. In spite of failure, keep going. If a new road has to be taken, then take it. If you are too tired to go on and choose to give up, then take a break. But, get back onto the road of life, even if you have to crawl. You will face pain in this life and you will survive. You will confront failure, but with perseverance, patience, and faith, you will succeed. There will always be good days to savor and bad days to learn from; but every day will come and go. Don't let a day go past without taking what ever you can get from that day.

No life is set in concrete. A poor person today can be a rich person tomorrow. A homeless person today can have nice home tomorrow. A student today can be a scholar tomorrow. A homebody today can be a world traveler tomorrow. There is no limit to what you can achieve. Start with faith and move forward.

➢ *Define the problem*
➢ *Make choices*

> ➤ *Set goals*
> ➤ *Do it*

Challenge yourself and challenge the world. Everything you need is right here. Find it, take it, use it, and live the life that you are entitled to.

Chapter 10
I Don't Like Myself

✦

Are you completely satisfied with yourself? I mean, satisfied with everything about you? Do you hate your legs or your nose? Are you too fat, too thin, too short, or too tall? Is your hair too straight or too curly? Do you yell too much? Are you too shy? The list goes on.

If you are really honest with yourself, you will answer that question with a big fat, no! Few people are truly satisfied with every single aspect of themselves. We are all going to find something in our physical self or in our inner self that we just don't like.

What ever it is that you don't like about yourself or wish you could change, may not be as bad as you might think. But, what you think is what is important, because that is what is real; at least to you. You may barely weigh a hundred pounds, but if you think you look fat, then you're fat. That is your reality.

You have the power to change any belief or feeling you have about yourself. It isn't easy to change the beliefs you have been carrying around about yourself, probably for a very long time, but it can be done. It is about learning to love yourself, even with all of your imperfections. It is changing what can be changed and learning to accept what cannot be changed. We are all familiar with the popular verse; *'Lord, help me to change the things that can be changed, the courage to accept the things that can't, and the wisdom to know the difference.'* And that verse is so true. But, changing the things that can be changed has to be things you want to change. The change has to start with you and with the beliefs that you have about yourself. **Change your thoughts and change what you believe.**

The changes you want to make will begin with you acknowledging the problem. You have to know what you want to change. You have to know what it is you don't like about you, and then, you have to be honest and decide if it is something that can realistically be changed. In this day and age most anything can be changed as far as physical appearance goes, but, inner changes may be more of a challenge.

Next, you will set a goal. What will you have to do to make the changes you desire? It may be that you won't have to change anything at all except your own beliefs and feelings about your perceived problem. For instance, if you don't care that you are overweight, but your family is bugging you to lose weight, then the problem isn't your weight, the problem is your family and their perception of your weight. In other words, it is their problem. But, since they have indirectly involved you and it bothers you, you are going to have to deal with it.

Dealing with the problem may be nothing more then changing your perception of the problem. You have to realize that your feelings are as important as the next person. If someone thinks you are overweight, but you don't feel overweight, then why should their beliefs be more important than yours? Why should you validate their reality? What makes their view right? If someone thinks you're fat, but you don't think you're fat, than you're not fat. That's the bottom line. You are not fat because you don't see yourself as fat, you don't feel fat, and you are happy with your weight. Your feelings and beliefs are just as important and just as real as anyone else's. You can set a goal to deal with those irritating people or you can move on and allow them to deal with the issue themselves.

On the other hand, you could be so overweight that it is causing a health issue. Maybe you don't care that you are so overweight that you might die. You have choices to make. Beliefs may have to be changed or reexamined. Look at your life realistically. The final choice of which road you will travel will be yours. Remember the Lords prayer. And, I'll repeat it again because it says so much. *Lord, help me to change the things that can be changed, the courage to accept the things that can't and the wisdom to know the difference.*

That goes for anything negative other people may think about you. Your feelings are just as real and just as valid as theirs. No one can tell you what you are or should be. You are what you think you are and what you want to be. Any changes made to you, have to be made by you, and only because it is something you choose to do.

Your happiness and self acceptance should be your first priority. For instance, say you make forty thousand dollars a year and you are very content with your life and with your income. Now, maybe your friends or family perceive forty thousand a year in the poverty range, and so, see you as poor. Their perceptions of your financial condition should mean nothing to you, if you are happy and satisfied with where you are at. On the other hand, if forty thousand dollars a year is not enough and you are just not satisfied with it, then change it. Set goals that will propel you toward a larger income. Start with baby steps until you are moving toward what you want out of life financially. It's all about you, your happiness, and what you want and need out of life to be successful.

The same holds true for the children in your life. Of course, children will have to function within your framework until they are old enough to make their own choices. Still, children should be encouraged to strive for their optimum happiness. Teach children to work toward goals that will make them happy and will foster self love in them. Give them skills that they can, and hopefully will, use later in life.

You don't like yourself? Are you any different than anyone else? Do you dream about being a self confident, socialite, prince or princes, fluttering through life like a butterfly, never experiencing the stress, wants and discontent of the average person? Well dream on.

Even the most glamorous and prestigious of us has issues about themselves. Why do you think plastic surgeons are so fat with wealth? Why do you think people spend millions on psychotherapy? They are doing just what you and I are doing. They are changing things they don't like about themselves and adding what they think will make them happy.

There are no real princesses out there, except for Cinderella, who had to make changes that pushed her forward to the life she wanted (and deserved.) There was beauty (and the beast) who had to change her perception of her situation; and then she was able to see that she had indeed found true happiness. The little mermaid made huge changes before she found true happiness. And you will too, once you decide what you need to be truly happy and set your goals toward achieving it.

Don't panic about the 'how to' part of it; that is the fun, exciting adventure. How will you get to where you want to be? What will you do? Who will come with you? What obstacles will you encounter along the way? All I can say is, "*let the games begin.*"

Instead of thinking that you do not like yourself, your personality, your nose, your hair, your life in general, now you can think in terms of what am I willing to do about it? What plan of action will I implement toward fully loving myself and achieving my goal of happiness?

What you believe is what is real. Your beliefs are the control center of your life. If your beliefs are causing unhappiness in your life then you have the power to change those thoughts and beliefs. You cannot change the way you look at things in one day. These beliefs have probably been the center of your life for years. Take as long as you feel you need to understand the root of your beliefs and to change those beliefs into something positive for you.

Take baby steps. Set goals and find ways to make them happen. If you fail or have a set back, just get up and start again. Remember, if you fall down seven times, get up eight. And keep getting up until you have accomplished the goals that will propel you through life and take you to where you want to be. Anything you choose to change can be changed back, if you decide the changes were not what you really wanted or needed. Your choices are not set in concrete. Life is fluid and change is a healthy part of life.

Loving yourself should be as natural as it was the day you were born. As we grow and have interactions with friends, family, enemies, spouses, and co-workers, our beliefs about ourselves become tangled with their beliefs about us, and soon we are a tangled mess of everyone's ideas of how we should be. This can be very confusing, as each person sees you differently. You will never be able to please everyone. But, you can learn to please yourself. Some people will love you, others will hate you. Someone may think you are cute as a button and others may think less. Loving you, over time, changes from a natural state to one that needs to be nurtured.

You are who you think you are. You are a garden of all of your experiences. You are special. Love yourself so you can treat yourself the way you deserve to be treated and others will also treat you the way you deserve to be treated.

You are unique and you are obligated to love yourself. You will do more for yourself, for your family, and for those you care about, when you have learned to love and accept yourself. You will achieve more in life when you realize you deserve everything you desire. When you love yourself, getting what you need is easy, achievable, and even fun.

Learning to love you can be an exciting adventure. Set goals. Nothing about your goals should be considered silly. Look into the mirror, everyday, or even two or three times a day, until you've said one thousand times, "I love me." Or, "my nose is beautiful." Or, "I am the best mother ever." You can say anything you want about yourself, weather it's true or not, as long as it is something you want to learn to believe about yourself. Take a note pad and write down hundreds of wonderful things about yourself, nothing negative, everything has to be positive and uplifting. Write things about yourself that you wish were true. Nothing is off limits in your search for loving the most important person you know. ***You.***

Chapter 11

Finding Me

✦

In this high tech world of computers and electronic gadgets, even right down to the newest toys for newborns, we can sometimes forget who we are. In this competitive world where both women and men compete for the best and highest paying jobs, we forget what we really believe in. In this life, where it is not uncommon for people to work long hours, we can easily become overwhelmed with life and forget about the most important person, *me*.

The world is a mass of technology, but humans remain human. In order to be successful at this we have developed a series of personalities that we use in this chaotic world. We call these different personalities roles and everyone has a series of roles that they use everyday.

Children take on roles such as friend, sibling and student. Adults take on more highly complex roles. These include such roles as teacher, parent, friend, lover, spouse, or employee, just to name a few.

Sometimes we are aware of the roles that we are choosing and other times these personalities just emerge when we need them. Every face we wear is meant to protect or support us in what ever situation we are in. Our many different roles and faces help us to cope. The roles we play and the faces we wear change daily, depending on our mood or how we perceive the situation we are in at any given moment.

Our hidden faces are one of our many tools of success. Of course, you wouldn't take your mommy personality to work and you wouldn't take your work personality home. If your goal is to become president of a company you certainly wouldn't use your mommy words at a board meeting. The faces we wear everyday are us in different modes, be it at work, home, family outing, or a business deal.

We are designed to adjust, to cope, and to change with each task we are involved in at any given moment in time. This is a good and versatile feature of human beings. Being aware of this can be a powerful tool for you. Every person has the ability to tap into this glorious feature of the personality, thus giving you the power to cope with any situation you are faced with. The secret is to decide when you want to use each unique aspect of yourself. Sometimes you may have to take a look at the situation you are in and become who you need to be at that given moment. If you are faced with a difficult situation, take a deep breath, and tap into the person you need to be to cope, then do it.

You have the ability to be successful at everything you want to do because you have the ability to relate to each situation that comes your way. You can be reserved and quite if you have to be. You can be aggressive and assertive if needed. You can be nurturing. Have faith in your ability to choose the right role for the right situation. Without this ability it would be very difficult to go to work and back home again, or to be a parent one moment and a lover the next.

Do become aware of all of your personal changes through out the day. Become aware of when you are shy or when you are more assertive or aggressive. All of these behaviors blend together to make up who you are. Use each aspect of your varied personality as you need to and choose the one that will benefit you at any given time.

Open yourself to all of your human possibilities and capabilities. Open yourself to life and what it has to offer. Open yourself to every aspect of who you are or who you want to be. Become aware of the power you possess within you.

You are unique and each aspect of your personality is unique. You have the ability to change and stretch yourself to meet every situation you are faced with, thus, giving you the power to achieve the greatest successes possible. There is nothing you can't accomplish, because you have so many tools to choose from in achieving your goals and dreams.

Everything you need to succeed in life is here, available for your use at any time you choose to take it. It may be something as simple as reading a book or talking to a friend. It could be more complicated such as making a life change.

> ➤ *Find what you need*
> ➤ *Take it*
> ➤ *Use it*

What you need will always be here. Nothing is out of reach when you are willing to make it a part of your journey. Life is full of gifts, put here for your use, don't pass these treasures up. The ability to change roles in a seconds notice is one of your gifts, use it to your advantage. Open your eyes, open your heart, and take your gifts.

Chapter 12

Alienation And Loneliness

✦

In the course of a busy week there are going to be times when you will become alienated from your spouse, your friends, your kids, and even yourself. The number of friends, co-workers, or romantic interests you have doesn't matter when it comes to feeling alone.

At some point the reality of eight or sixteen-hour shifts, daily pressures, unpaid bills, school responsibilities, and daily chores and commitments will catch up with you, and you will feel overwhelmed and alone. No one is going to offer to take the kid's to soccer, do your laundry, or pay your bills; they have their own burdens to bear. You are alone.

Everyday you are stretched mentally and physically by co-workers, children, and spouses; most of these people are just as stretched as you are. Every minute of your time is soaked up caring for children, running errands, working, living your goals and dreams, and the list goes on. You are bombarded daily by a hundred different needs, responsibilities, and temperaments. You have unending obligations to family, friends, and even the stray dog you took in to find a home for. With all of this going on it doesn't seem you would have the time to feel alienated and alone, but you do, and you are.

A result of this constant pull on your life (from every direction possible) is that you will either become stronger or the harsh reality, you will snap. Physically and mentally you will come apart.

Snapping has benefits. Your mind (that has been inflating like a balloon) will suddenly pop. You will experience a well deserved rest and a breath of fresh air. Snapping is, in a sense, a form of giving up. But, before giving up, stop and take a good long look at your life and what is going wrong. Take a look at your faith and question why it is not working for you. I think you will find that you have not given up, but have only temporarily stepped off the path of life. You are on a mini vacation. Now is the time to reevaluate your faith, your goals, and your dreams. Examine your life and make sure everything is in order. Look for obstacles or changes in your situation, anything that may be a clue as to why your life has become so unbearable or unmanageable. It may be that you have to adjust or change your goals for right now.

So, what do you do? How do you stop the balloon from popping? First, acknowledge that you have come to the end, that you have reached your breaking point. Affirm your faith. Tune into your feelings, you may have something troubling you that you were not aware of. Become aware of any changes in your life; look for even tiny changes that may be causing a problem. Maybe you feel overwhelmed by your goals; have you set them too high? That's okay, redefine your goals and take smaller steps. Taking a serious look at your life and where you are at right now, both mentally and physically, is important, because it will give you the power to make instant changes that are needed in your life right now.

Let's make some quick temporary changes. How about a week-end getaway? Maybe all you need is a long, hot bath, with a cold drink and lots of chocolate. A walk along the beach or around the park can be refreshing. Take your spouse or a close friend out to dinner. Ship the kids to grandma or Aunt Sue for the week-end. Meditate. Write. Make a list of possible new goals or changes in your life. Sign up for an aerobics class. The list is endless and can be adapted to any budget or time frame. You may need several doses of quick changes. Do what you have to do. Depend on your faith to pull you through. Don't return to the front lines until you're ready. Put reality on the back burner for a minute. Concentrate on you.

And what is the reality? The reality is that you can make it, no matter how alone or scared you feel or really are. The reality is you have faith, perseverance, patience, and the ability to make things happen. The reality is your life is a whirlwind of relationships, daily chores, eight-hour shifts, soccer practice, and loneliness. The reality is that you are a strong person with goals and dreams. You are writing a story that isn't always going have happy chapters, but each chapter will always leave you with something, be it greater strength, more understanding, new skills, or the potential for future success. Your life will be full of challenges and successes, both of which build on each other.

What is giving up or mentally snapping? It takes the form of drug abuse, alcoholism, suicide, mental breakdowns, depression, and the abuse of self, family or friends. When you become overwhelmed with life you began to feel alone, scared, and alienated from others. This signals danger, because this is the time when snapping can be set in motion, if you allow it to.

Have you already snapped? Do you feel so overwhelmed and alone that you can barely get through a day? You can barely get out of bed? There are things you can do to start feeling good again. There are things you can do that will allow you to move on. Some of your choices may include.

- ➢ *Therapy*
- ➢ *Exercise*
- ➢ *Family*
- ➢ *Friends*
- ➢ *Time away*
- ➢ *Meditation*
- ➢ *The spa*
- ➢ *Your minister or rabbi*
- ➢ *A special self help book*
- ➢ *Writing*
- ➢ *Visualization*

Your choices are endless. Take your time and decide what will work best for you. Acknowledge that things aren't right. Most important, you have to want to get back on track again and you have to be ready, physically and mentally. And last, you have to make plans and set a goal on how you are going to achieve this.

Depending on how much control you have lost, determines how much help you will need to gain control again, and to get back onto the road of life. If you are just feeling alienated, mad at the world, and disillusioned by your life in general, then you can pretty much determine where you want to go from where you are at, and with time and patience, get there.

If, on the other hand, you have lost all control, and have no idea where you are or where you want to be, then, you must seek professional help. I will assume that if you are able to read this book that you still have a certain amount of control. Choose someone you feel comfortable with to talk to, someone who can help you move on. If getting professional help isn't possible then seek out a trusted friend or someone from your church or temple. There are numerous organizations that offer assistance to people for little or no money, tap into these agencies. You may have to do a little leg work to find the right one, but the search will be well worth your time.

There are endless options open to you, but first you have to determine what your needs are. You are never static. There is always an answer, always a way back to life's main path. The trick is to find it. Now is the time to rely on your faith. Look at your life and look at your options, then make choices about where you are going and where you want to be. The choice is yours. The answers are here.

Feeling isolated and alone can make you more susceptible to giving up. There will be times when you will become so discouraged that you will wonder if it is all even worth it. And, I will tell you that, yes, it is all worth it. The good, the bad, the ups, and the downs, are all needed to write your story.

No matter how bad life may seem when you are at your lowest; life is always worth coming back to. What about the children or grandchildren you may someday have, is that worth waiting for? Are you raising a child who may someday find a cure for cancer? Have you experienced the ultimate love of a soul mate? Have you bought that dream car? All of these treasures are worth holding on for. How about a trip to the Grand Canyon, camping inside a cave in Utah, hiking along the Colorado River, traveling to a foreign country, experiencing the mystery and beauty of ancient art? There are new discoveries to be seen and felt in this world. There is so much to see, and do, and be proud of. We need to be alive to enjoy all that awaits us, physically, mentally, and spiritually.

Loneliness and isolation can be defeated. Don't scare off your family and friends by dumping all of your emotional issues on them. Remember, they have their own issues. You must become intuitive and sensitive to your fellow travelers and be able to distinguish which people are open to helping you, those you may be able to help, and when you will have to go it alone.

There are negative and positive ways to deal with isolation and loneliness. You will more then likely tap into both. Be open to tapping into ways that are not characteristic of you. Make choices that may be risky. Don't be afraid to experiment with options. All of these choices may prove to be just what you need to move on with your life. Challenge yourself. And, go ahead and feel sorry for yourself. Feel anger toward those you feel have more than you. Dislike people (for the moment) who have life handed to them on a gold platter. Envy those who get ten hours of sleep while you get barely two. All of these feelings are valid as you plan your strategy for moving on.

Get a notebook and write down all of your feelings, both negative and positive. Have you accomplished too little? Are there things you wished you had done differently? Have people you loved and trusted turned on you? Write it down. Are your kids thoughtless and lazy? Is your spouse unloving and insensitive to your needs? Write it down. Put all of your feelings on paper. Now you have something concrete to look at. This list will eventually be broken down to reflect your priorities. You can only move one foot at a time; and now is the time to start. Even one foot will move you forward, toward where you want to be.

It is important to keep your feelings and actions separate. Feelings are always okay; actions may not always be okay. It is never okay to hurt another person, physically or mentally. We will, as we travel through life, hurt others, but hurting others intentionally is not okay. So, you must separate your actions from your feelings. Analyze your situation before you act.

Seek out someone like yourself, someone you can identify with. This person will probably have life experiences similar to your own. Maybe you are both single parents, or you both may be Jewish, or both college students. Look for something that may bind you together. And, that my friend is a start. You may choose not to have any friends, and that's okay. Having a special someone is helpful and makes the journey easier, but is never a necessity.

Every day your plan of action may change, just as your mood and feelings will change; keep the flow moving from day to day. You don't have to be lonely and isolated from others. One day you may want to seek out a co-employee or another person, another day you may choose to be alone. Any choice you make is okay as long as you are moving forward. Do not allow yourself to become static and stuck in one place. Move on and move toward your dreams and goals. Loneliness and isolation are just temporary moments that will come and go as you journey forward.

Many people resort to a fantasy world (visualization) as a way of coping with loneliness. Daydreaming about that guy at work or dreaming of driving a Rolls Royce is okay, and can be a great release; but don't allow it to replace real life situations. Use visualization to compliment real life and to move you forward. You may be shy; visualize about talking to others until you can do it in real life. You may have a crush on the guy at work, visualize about talking to him and then do it. Visualization is safe and gives you a chance to experiment before doing the real thing. Visualization is a way of coping with loneliness and isolation.

Visualization is not meant to cut you off from reality, but to enhance that reality. Visualization gives you the opportunity to experience events before they actually happen. Use the power of visualization and enjoy it.

There is no right or wrong way of dealing with loneliness and isolation, tap into ideas that have worked for you in the past, experiment with new behaviors and ideas, and take risks. Isolation and loneliness will come and go as you move through life. The secret is to keep moving forward; do not become immobilized.

Your feelings of isolation and loneliness will most certainly affect those closest to you; be aware of this. You may become cranky or overly sensitive, be prepared to deal with these behaviors. Remember to ask for help if you need it. Asking for help is not a sign of weakness and will allow you to move on quicker.

Isolation and loneliness are normal feelings we all experience. How you cope will be unique to you. And remember, this to will pass.

Chapter 13

When Everything Goes Wrong

✦

You have opened yourself to all of the ideas that have been presented to you. You have tapped into and are now working at using your faith, perseverance, and patience. You have looked deep within yourself and are now in the process of learning to accept who you are. You are opening up to all of the possibilities available to you. You have set goals and dreamed dreams, giving them the power of life. You have asked for, and are now getting, the respect you are entitled to. So what's the problem? Why is everything still going wrong?

Things are not going wrong, things are going right. You are growing, learning, and moving forward, but, all of your problems have not magically disappeared. You are learning ways of dealing with the problems that are a part of your life. You are learning ways to live with or change these problems; but they haven't just gone away. As you grow and as your thoughts change, you will begin to cope with all of the issues and challenges in your life in a positive and productive way.

Your life will become enriched as your dreams take shape. Your life and your beliefs will change as you set and achieve your goals. Your problems do not disappear, they are still here. However, you may now see them in a different light.

You can never forget the poverty you lived in, or the abuse you took from an ex spouse, or your struggles as a single parent, but you will overcome these problems and you will remember them as you move forward. These memories of past hardships and pains will motivate you to continue to move forward, and will give you the strength to help others on your journey. The past influences the future.

You are in the process of taking baby steps toward the life you want. Do not expect to much to soon; it is a journey. In time, if you stick to your faith, perseverance, and patience, everything will fall together. The process is ongoing and you are evolving, things will go wrong. But you now have the tools you need that will move you forward as you face the challenges and struggles of life. The key is to move forward; utilizing all of the skills you have learned. You are still facing issues and hardships, and you will. Life is ongoing. Continue the journey.

A child begins school with no knowledge of reading. At the end of first grade she is beginning to read, but she has limited knowledge in what she is able to read. She will continue reading, harder and harder books, and with time the skill will become more advanced, until years later she will reach the final goal of a perfect reader. So it is with you, you are a beginner. You will have to practice and use your skills. Unlike reading, you will never reach a final goal. You are changing and evolving, and your dreams and goals will continually change. Your life will continually change. Learning new skills and using old ones that have been successful for you in the past is essential to your continued growth.

Something all human beings have in common is that no-one, no matter how perfect their lives may seem, are without problems. The second thing most people have in common is that they are finding ways to cope with their own life situations. Some in positive ways and some in negative ways; everyone is writing a story.

Your main concern should be your own life story and your own situation. So, how do you deal with adversity in your life? First, you have to evaluate what the problem is. Put the problem on the table. You don't have to be honest with others if you don't want them to know your personal business, but do be as honest with yourself as possible. Your perception may not be accurate, but it will be your honest evaluation, later you will be able to see your situation in a different light

You may be familiar with the saying; *you can't see the forest for the trees.* Slowly chop the trees down. At first, your perception of a major problem may not be as accurate as you might think, so, be open to other possibilities.

Next, be open to the vast pool of options available for you to choose from. Some of your options and choices will be extreme, and others may not be noticeable to anyone but you. You are going to have to be strong and take a stand once you make a choice. You may choose to talk to a relative you haven't spoken to in years, or you may choose to move to another town, or sell a car. There will always be choices and options when solving your problems. Look at all of them, and then do it.

Let's say you want to lose weight. First, you evaluate the situation and determine that you are over weight and want to lose "x" amount of pounds. Next, explore all of the options available to you. Some ideas might include cutting fast foods, eliminating soft drinks or starting an exercise program. Look at all of your options and set a goal that will work for you.

Now you are ready to reach for your target goal of losing weight. You may not be one hundred percent successful and that's okay, just start again. Keep going. It's about not giving up once a decision to do something has been made. And, if you do decide you don't want to continue to lose weight, then that is okay. You are not a failure. Life is not static and things can and do change.

Act, this is a major step; you have evaluated your situation, looked at your options, set goals, geared yourself up for success by tuning into your faith, and now your must act. Do something. No matter how small, you must take the first step. Weather you want to lose weight or pull yourself through something tragic; you must be willing to take action. No situation is so tragic that you can't take that first step toward healing. Every story has an ending no matter how tragic, no matter how life-shattering. So, take the first step and see where you go.

The two most devastating events that could happen in a life would most likely be the loss of a child or a loved one, or an accident or illness that leaves you or someone you love physically or mentally shattered. Then there is all of the major events in-between. Is living through such tragic events really possible?

Yes, I think it is possible to not only live through these events, but to come out a stronger person. It is all a matter of getting past the event, accepting that it happened, and deciding what you are going to do to pull your life back together. In every bad event comes something good. There are people who lose their children and in the sad possess help hundreds more. The mother, who lost her son to AIDS, started the Ryan White Foundation, that helps millions. The group, MADD, helps others who have lost their children to drunk drivers. Children, who die suddenly in accidents or from illnesses, have parents who had the strength to donate the organs of their child to others in need, thus helping to save the lives of countless others. Remember, horrible, bad, unbearable events, no matter how devastating, can have positive effects with the power to touch others, who have also experienced a devastating event in their lives. Life can hurt. Some chapters in your life are going to hurt more than others, but you will survive and you will move on.

Not coping is a way of coping. Suicide is a choice. Drugs are a choice. Not all choices are going to be positive. Surviving is a choice. You have suffered a great loss, but life forces us to make a choice on how we will handle what has been handed to us. This will end a chapter in your life. The next chapter of your life may go on for a long time as you learn to live with your choices and learn to deal with your loss. It may not be a happy chapter in your life, but a necessary one. You will survive. Your life has taken a drastic turn, but you will deal with it, because you have within you an abundance of strength and you have your faith.

It doesn't matter what the traumatic event is, it could be a divorce, a child out of control, a family issue, a sick child, or your own illness. No problem should be considered small. All traumatic events have a major impact on your life and always on the lives of others.

Yes, you will grieve and go through a period of depression when adversity hits and that is okay. You will wonder if life is worth all the pain. Allow yourself time to experience all of your feelings of anger, grief, despair, and emptiness, then move on when you feel you are ready.

REMEMBER:

- *Evaluate the problem*
- *Open yourself to options available to you*
- *Make choices*
- *Set goals*
- *Open yourself to your faith, patience, and perseverance*
- *Act*

Of course everything seems easier on paper. The healing possess won't be as easy as completing the steps on a list, but it will be a start. There is always the beginning; and nothing will happen until you start.

This is the first real step toward healing. You must start. You will begin the process with anger, fear, and a total feeling of loss. You will cry, scream, and grieve. Your reactions to any event will be determined by the event. Go with the flow of your anger or grief until you feel ready to put your life back together. Don't rush or push yourself. Your own body rhythms will tell you when you are ready to act. Have faith in yourself and in your ability to move on; and then begin the healing process.

Life will go on. Things will go wrong. Events will take place in your life that will have a negative impact on you. You will survive with the tools you have on hand and with the skills you have acquired to help you cope. You will turn to these tools and skills, and realize that you are able to move forward, because you have what it takes to survive.

You are a survivor. You are strong. You have the ability to move on even in the worst of times and so you see that yes, your life is still full of problems and that will continue. You now have skills that will help you cope and motivate you to move forward. Not every choice will be a good choice, not every endeavor will be successful, and that's when you use the knowledge you have learned to find other answers and sources available to you. Life will move on and you will move on with it. Know and believe that you have the resources you need, if you choose to use them.

Every step you take in life is a step toward your goals and dreams. Every success and every failure affects you, your family, and all of those close to you. Every choice you make will alter your life and the lives of those you love. Every book you read is a choice, every person you allow into your world is a choice, and everything you learn and use from that book or from those people will move you forward.

Don't expect immediate results. What you need will come. Continue to dream, set goals, and believe that everything you do is a step forward. Teach your children to dream, set goals, and move forward. If children learn these concepts when they are young, they will already be on the path of happiness and success. And isn't that a huge goal of many people, to send your little vessels into the world already equipped for success and happiness?

- *Keep moving forward*
- *Dream*
- *Set goals*
- *Have faith*
- *Patience*
- *Perseverance*
- *Give to life*
- *Take from life*
- *Write your story*

Nothing in your life is going wrong; everything is going right, because you are making it right, with your faith, your willingness to take risks and your strength in facing challenges. Live life to the fullest; believe in and take all of your blessings gracefully. Every day take one step closer toward your goal of happiness and success.

Chapter 14

It's Too Much, I Can't Take It

✦

It's too much, I can't take it, I can't do it anymore. Life is so overwhelming. I can barely get to work, and when I am at work, I hate it. I can't control the kids. The house is a nightmare. I'm tired, overwhelmed, lonely, lost and depressed. The bills are too far behind to care anymore, or worse, I'm about to lose everything. I can't sleep at night and I can't get up in the morning. All I can do anymore is cry. I hate my life. There is no joy in living.

Wow, we are talking extreme, the end of the world. A Life that is too harsh to even live anymore. And that is what this chapter is about, the extreme.

Most of you are probably not at this point. This is the point where real intervention is called for. Get medical attention as fast and as soon as possible; this will be your stating point in getting yourself back into balance. Nothing can be accomplished if you are so far out of balance that even breathing is painful.

How you got to this breaking point doesn't matter. What does matter is that you know you are there and you need to get back into balance. Life is not over. You may be at the end of the road, but u-turns are still possible.

Most of you reading this book are still functioning. Yes, you may be feeling totally out of balance and about to give up, but you are still in the game or you wouldn't be reading this book. And being in the game gives you both choices and challenges to get back on track. It can be done. You will succeed because you have your faith. Right now, at this point in your life, you may feel like things are horrible, and they may really be. Sit down, take a deep breath and put your life into focus. Maybe things aren't as bad as you might think. Or, maybe there are options you haven't considered or choices you haven't even tried yet.

Set new goals. Take tiny steps until you feel like you are in control again. Let's take a scenario, nothing to overwhelming, but the steps will be the same for any life situation you encounter. Let's say you are completely burned out. You have been working double shifts just to stay above water. The kids are totally out of control. You are feeling sad and alone. Okay, let's begin the healing possess.

Sit down, anywhere you feel comfortable, and take as long as you need (even days) to get a complete picture of your situation. Really examine what is going on in your life. Look at every aspect of your life, your kids, your spouse, your job, your leisure activities, and your deepest feelings. As the minutes, hours, and days tick away, you are going to get a clearer picture of what is really happening in your life. Once the emotional impact has passed and you are able to visualize your situation, changes in your thinking will magically begin.

How you viewed a problem, in the beginning, may seem manageable once you have had time to clear your mind and focus on the real issues. You are unconsciously changing the situation by how you are looking at it. Once it is down to a manageable size it can be more effectively dealt with. Now is the time to make changes, while your mind is clear and the problem does not seem as threatening. You can now look at options.

Stay focused on what the problem is and on what you want or need to keep yourself in balance. No problem is too large to handle. Change your thoughts and take action. You cannot change anyone else, only yourself, so all of the changes have to start with you.

Now, back to our scenario, you are burned out, both at work and at home. The kids are out of control and you're feeling sad and alone. Think about your options, some of your choices might include simple changes such as pacing yourself at work or requesting less stressful duties. Maybe you can ask for extra days off or a shift adjustment.

Maybe it isn't work at all. After looking over your situation you realize you are just drained, both physically and mentally and just need some time away. Once you have identified some of your issues, you can begin to take steps toward changing your situation.

Don't be afraid to make changes. Take control of your life. Start with small changes that will make even a small difference. Test the waters before making any huge life changes. And, remember, you might have to take some risks. Decide how much risk you are willing to take, then make choices that will reflect that risk.

The kids are out of control, maybe, maybe not. Maybe they are just being kids. Do they need firmer limits? Or, do you need to loosen up a little? Maybe you can talk to them or learn to ignore behaviors that aren't all that bad, just irritating. These are only samples of choices available to you. It is up to you to determine what will work for you, considering the personality of your family.

You are sad and lonely. Change that, go out more, make plans with the kids, look at all of your blessings and feel how truly blessed you are. Sadness is within you and can be easily changed with nothing more than an attitude adjustment.

You may be searching for new meaning in life. You are ready to give up your house, car, bank account, and move to another country to work with the poor. This would fall under major life changes. Do it; but first stop, analyze, and make choices.

When you are contemplating a major life change, you are going to have to seriously look at your new goals and decide if this is what you really want. Sometimes when we become overwhelmed we jump into choices that might not be right for us. So take time to look at your situation and make sure you are not just running away from your pain. If you have analyzed your situation and know that this is what you really want, then set your goals, make choices, and do it.

Every choice, every obstacle, every goal, has the potential for success, but also there is the risk of things not working out the way you planned. This is not a failure, but only a wrong turn. You might have to turn yourself around and take another route (which would be a new goal). Be aware that the chance of this happening is possible. Setting new goals is not something to be feared, but to be viewed as a new adventure, with new outcomes.

The issue of what is happening in your life will have to be faced, no matter how painful. Don't deny the existence of the problem. Every issue or problem in your life must be acknowledged before any work can be done on it. You don't want to deny the problem; you want to define the problem.

Remember, what we have explored are just scenarios, real problems and issues are infinite. What is yours? Look at your problems and know that you have an abundance of faith and an abundance of choices; you don't have to be in any situation you don't want to be in. But, to get out of some situations will take some work on your part.

Any situation that is too overwhelming to face alone requires help. Get the help you need. Seeking out help is another positive option open to you. The help you seek doesn't have to be from a professional, it can be a relative, a friend, or even an uninvolved outsider.

The steps for moving forward when you feel overwhelmed are steps toward an inner healing.

REMEMBER:

➢ *Sit down and breathe*
➢ *Focus on the problem*
➢ *Examine your situation*
➢ *Visualize your situation*
➢ *Change your thoughts*
➢ *Look at your options*
➢ *Set goals*
➢ Act

You are unique and your situation is unique. Your choices are infinite. You never have to be where you don't want to be. Use your goal setting skills, dream big, and move forward.

Chapter 15

Changing Lanes In Life

✦

Things are going pretty good. You have the house of your dreams. A prestigious job, the kids are excelling in school and at home they are helpful, considerate, and well behaved. You and your spouse have achieved a level of understanding and communication that has expanded your relationship. You have stabilized and are now living your dreams, moving toward your goals, and paying off bills. Things are okay. But, you decide you want a change. For some reason you're feeling restless and want something new from life.

Let's divide life changes into two categories, those who know what they want but are not sure how to get there, and those who want a change but are not sure of what they want. This new life change you desire can be anything, from a restless yearning to explore another side of life, to retiring, quitting your current job, divorce, getting married, selling your house, or moving to another country. There is no limit to what your desire for change may be. The change you are seeking may be something small or it can be a huge, drastic life change; one that will alter your entire life course.

The thought of a complete life change is exciting, but the road can be challenging. It starts with a dream, a goal, and faith, just like all of the other choices you have made in your life. Complete life changes are just bigger and more challenging than every day changes. Life changes occur when people change and so their wants and needs change. Remember, life is fluid and can change at any moment.

The good news is that you can go where ever you want to go and change what ever you want to change in your life. The question is how are you going to do it? Of course, you will start with goals and plans, just like when you graduated from high school, got married, or had children. You are embarking on a new adventure and so will need a whole new set of goals.

With life changes you will face mountains, fears, and doubts. But also, you will experience a chilling thrill as your new life unfolds. Still, unless you are very adventurous and aren't afraid of risk, there will be steps that you will have to take to prepare yourself for the journey. Let's do a scenario. You want to quit your job and dedicate all of your time to that great novel you have always wanted to write. It would be nice if you could quit your job and plop down at the computer. More realistically, you will probably want to start with a definite plan and set definite goals. Your goals are your map of where you want to be and how you will get there.

No matter what life change you are considering, you will have to plan and then evaluate that plan. Then have faith that the change you want to make is the right one for you and that it will elevate you to a higher level of where you want to be in life.

Visualize your new life choice. Make it a positive experience. Get yourself excited about the changes that will happen in your life.

And for those who like to just leap forward. Go for it. Unconsciously, you will be making plans. Don't waste any time if you are willing to face what ever obstacles you might encounter on the road you have chosen. Do it. Have faith, persevere, and have patience as your journey unwinds. The worst that can happen is you will have to move back to where you were before you took the big risk. You may end up back to where you started, but you took the challenge and you learned and prospered from the experience. You will never know what you can do if you don't do it. And we all know that side trips are a lot more fun than just traveling on the same road.

Most people prefer to move slow as new life challenges unwind. Let's start with those people who know what they want to do and are ready to work on how they will achieve it. Sit down, preferably alone, in a quite spot where you are comfortable and let your brain think. Think about what you want to do and how it will affect you and those you love. Think about your anticipated life change, and even better, write it down. Write down the pros and cons of your choices. Write how important it is for you to take this risk in life; to venture onto this unknown journey. Is it something you really want to do? Are you willing to make major sacrifices if you have to? Are there others who will be affected by this life change? If so, how are you going to deal with that?

You might have children that are still very young, but you really want to travel to Africa and work in a refugee camp. Will you take the kid's with you? Are you willing to leave them with a family member? Or, will you have to postpone your dream for a few years until they are older? These are issues that will affect your choice and how you will go about achieving it. Can you postpone your dream for a few years? Or, will you take the kids with you? If you decide you want to go for it and take the kids with you, you will now be faced with other challenges. Where will the kids go to school? Where will you live? What role will the children have in your new life choice? And, of course, the list goes on. As you can see planning is a must in any drastic life change. Life changes are **always** possible, but plan, plan, plan, have goals and move forward.

You have asked yourself all of the questions that will open your eyes completely to the challenges ahead. You are now ready to act. You know what you want, and now you will have to plan on how you will achieve your new life goal. Your goals and dreams will be dependent on your faith. With any life change is a fear of the unknown; no matter how sure you are or how well planned the goal is; a big life change is scary. Stay grounded in your faith.

Plan, dream, pull everything together, then move forward, and don't stop once the gears have been set in motion. You will encounter doubts and even set backs. Life does not run smoothly all of the time. Not everything goes as planned, hopefully it will, but more then likely there will be stumbling blocks. Depend on your faith and keep moving. I cannot tell you how to get there, because with most life changes the journey is a mystery. I can only encourage you to utilize the tools you possess: faith, patience, and perseverance. Then, do it, do it, do it.

The second group of people who feel they need or want a change in their lives are those who feel something is changing inside of themselves. They know something is missing in their lives, but are uncertain of what it is. Again, you will have to sit down and think. Think about what you want. What are your dreams and goals? Who will be affected by the changes you make? Dig into your most inner thoughts and feelings and pull out what it is that is pushing you to seek more. Pull out those secret thoughts that will give you insight as to *why* you are seeking this change.

It is important to understand why you are making a change, so that your plans and goals will reflect this. Why do you want to change the security of what you are already familiar with? Why are you feeling restless? What is missing in your current life? The answer to these questions will give you the insight you need to make a final choice. You may decide you only have to make some small changes in your life to satisfy that craving for change. Or, you may decide to move forward with a complete life change, either choice is okay.

The most important issue you will have to think about is, *sacrifice.* How much are you willing to sacrifice to achieve your new goal? How much are you willing to give up or risk? Most life changes involve some sort of sacrifice. It may be the sacrifice of having less money, or having to sell your house, or having to give up the comforts you are familiar with. What ever the sacrifice is you are going to have to be willing to deal with it. Are you? If you are not willing to sacrifice then you are not ready for a major life change.

Taking risks, sacrificing, looking failure in the face, conquering challenges that will alter your entire life, these choices are all dependent on you. If you know what you want to do, then do it. If you are not sure, experiment before facing the final challenge. You make all the final choices. Do not be scared of life, but do be prepared to face life's challenges. A major life change is a choice, a goal, a dream. Do it and have faith. You are paving a new trail, with new challenges and possible loses, be well prepared.

There is no such thing as failure. Roads come to dead ends, roads close, or highways go into the sun. Life changes are new horizons with new challenges to conquer. Failure is not an option, not when you have abundant choices to work with.

Experimenting, taking risks, moving forward in the dark, these are all choices, and they all come with a lesson, but never constitute failure. If your first choice, or your second, or third, doesn't work out the way you planned, dreamed, or hoped, then turn down another road and start again.

Life is full of adventures, but you don't have the luxury of time. One gift life has not given to us is an abundance of time; so we cannot waste what little time we have been given. There are adventures out there to be lived; find one and jump in.

Life moves and curves in many different directions, giving us plenty of things to do to make our lives meaningful and exciting. If you are living and experiencing life then you are on the right track. A life change can be an exciting adventure. Life changes are an option open to anyone willing to take the risk and to anyone ready for a change.

Enjoy years of comfort in one secure spot, savoring the beauty in your own back yard. Or, be as fluid as a glass of water, moving through life and exploring many different adventures. It is your book, your story, your journey.

One group of people facing life changes that I didn't mention (I focused on those who desired change) are those who are forced into a life change due to some tragedy in their lives, such as job loss. These people face a different challenge. They weren't ready for a change and had no desire for change. Still, change is happening and must be dealt with.

Life moves in many different directions. An unplanned life change can certainly be a huge mountain to climb. But, as with everything we have talked about, you are still living life and challenges are a part of that life. Sometimes the most feared change can end up being the best thing that ever happened in your life.

Face the challenge, not in anger, scared, or defeated, but with the same vitality and lust for life that you would face any other challenge. The road of life can get bumpy. Get a firm grip on the steering wheel and set goals and plans that will reflect you new life. Becoming negative will only make the experience more painful. Face the challenge and turn it into something positive.

Embrace change. Planned or unplanned, change can be a thrilling adventure, if you allow it to be.

Chapter 16

Spiritual Growth

✦

Your spiritual journey begins from the inside. What you see with your heart is the spiritual part of you. Believing in a source that you can turn to when you need the power of something greater than yourself, is a part of your spiritual heritage. Nature is the physical part of the spiritual world. All of these are a part of your spiritual journey.

Do you belong to a temple or a church? Now is the time to connect to your religious roots in any way you feel comfortable. Read bible stories to your children or teach them ways that they can help others. Teach your children the values you want them to possess. These values can be anything you value yourself, such as honesty, kindness, helping others, or education. You don't have to be religious to connect to the spiritual part of yourself, and you don't have to belong to a temple or church to begin your spiritual journey.

Be open to the many ways you can learn to connect to your spiritual self. Religion is one way of achieving this. Open yourself to the possibilities that exist for you to choose from. Spiritual values are as important as the values we live by everyday. Spiritual values are the inner you. Spiritual values would include such values as:

- *Helping those less fortunate*
- *Kindness to others*

- *Caring for animals*
- *Respect for nature*
- *Understanding beyond drug addiction*
- *Compassion for the homeless*
- *Empathizing with the inner pain of others*

These are all a part of spiritual values. Material parts of our spiritual world include: Mountains, lakes, rivers, flowers, and butterflies, just to name a few. Teach children (nieces, nephews, grandchildren, your own children) to appreciate and respect these wonderful creations.

Take all of these elements and put them together to build a strong foundation for your spiritual growth. As you learn to understand and appreciate the beauty of the world, you will look less at the negative aspects of your life. As your spiritual self emerges, you will see and understand things about life, and about other people, you never knew before. You will gain a new understanding about the pain of others. You will begin to really appreciate how blessed your own life really is.

A basic law of the spiritual world is the belief that all you give, you will get back. If you plant weeds, you will reap weeds. If you plant roses, you will reap roses. Sometimes you have to give to others without expecting anything in return, not even a thank you. Others may be so overwhelmed with their own burdens that they cannot appreciate what you do for them. But, your reward will come, maybe in something as simple as an especially great day at the beach with your kids or friends.

Some gifts are small, others are large. Sometimes, a lot more times then you realize, gifts go right past you. Countless times people miss out on gifts because they did not realize it was a gift. You have to open up to every possibility that comes your way. Take the time to notice the gifts that befall you on a daily bases.

There will be times when you are just too tired to give anything of yourself to anyone, this is understandable and okay. Never force yourself, it will come naturally. Just remember that when you do have something to give, no matter how small, it will return to you many times over.

This isn't saying to let others take advantage of you. Sometimes others will mistake kindness for weakness and they will take advantage of it. Become aware of that danger, but do not let it stop you from giving to those who need your assistance along the road of life.

Do not become so giving that you become obsessed with it. There has to be a balance to everything. If you are naturally a giving person then you will have to become aware of that and balance it. Giving to others does not have to come in the form of money; it can be kind words, help, time, or just an everyday kindness. Do not think that your life has to become a series of helping everyone who is down and out. Yes, you will pass many people who need help, but remember; they are writing their own stories and are given the same opportunities in life as you are given. Do what you want to do or feel moved to do, then move on. Every act of kindness builds on other acts of kindness, from everyone.

One day my sister and I were driving to the store. A man was standing on the corner with a sign asking for money. I told my sister, "you should give something to him; it'll come back to you." So, she handed me a dollar and I handed it to the man. A few weeks later I received an unexpected check in the mail. I called my sister to tell her the good news.

Her reply was, "I thought something was supposed to come back to me, I was the one who gave the dollar to the man."

My reply, "No, you handed me the dollar, I gave it to the man." That was a cute story. The moral is to not expect anything. You are not going to be rewarded for every little kindness, but they do add up. And, on a lighter note, if you are giving someone money, make sure you personally hand the money to the person yourself.

We are all familiar with the story of the rich man who gave the beggar a gold piece worth a lot of money, and the poor man who gave the beggar one penny. The poor man was blessed and given a golden crown in heaven. The rich man demanded to know why the poor man was given a golden crown, and he was given nothing, when he gave a valuable gold piece and the poor man gave only a penny. And the Lord replied. "The poor man gave all he had."

Sometimes giving all you have may be an hour of your time once a month or giving a dollar to someone on a street corner. Most important, it is all in how much spirit you have when you give. You do not owe anyone anything and they don't owe you anything, not even a thank you, if they choose not to give it. Give with no expectation of a reward. Do not expect anything in return or you might be disappointed.

If you are having a really good month, the bills are paid, you have a few dollars in your pocket, your gas tank is full, your children have been double the joy they usually are, and you even have a special week-end planned, then by all means, give a little something to someone else, as a sort of thank you for your own good fortune. Remember, it will come back to you anyway. Take a good look at your life and become aware of what you may have already gotten back from all you have done for others. And don't look for just material rewards. Rewards come in a lot of different packages. Open yourself to the possibilities.

On a higher note, you may eventually not expect or want anything back for what you give to or do for others; just the act of your kindness will be payment enough. Compare it to a child getting potty trained (okay it's all I could think of.) At first, every time she goes to the potty, the small child expects a piece of gum or a piece of candy. Eventually, a kiss or verbal praise is enough, until finally; the satisfaction of being dry is all that is needed.

Keep in mind that you may be someone else's blessing. You could be someone else's vessel when they are in need spiritually, physically, mentally or financially. How many times has your vessel come in when you least expected it?

To be spiritually alive, and to truly appreciate life with all of its trials and rewards, you are going to have to look at life in a new light. Life is not about living each day satisfied that you managed to struggle through twenty-four hours. Life is an adventure to be lived; it is your personal story.

Spiritual values are also expressed in your kindness toward others. I don't mean to be nice day in and day out. If the guy at Mc Donald's doesn't fill your fries then go ahead and rant and rave. Being kind to others goes beyond putting up with people that irritate you. You are not a care bear. On television care bears are really cuddly, cute, and pukey nice. But, in real life people will irritate you. You will argue with people and maybe even curse them out. Conflict with others is unavoidable if you are human. There's the guy on the freeway that just flipped you off, the guy at the grocery store who won't honor your coupon, the kid who just ran over your best plant, the neighbor who constantly complains about your dog. Don't drive yourself crazy thinking you have to be nice all of the time to everyone, although, if possible, you should try to be nice to everyone anyway.

Being kind to others is being in tune with those who need you. There are people who may just need a smile or a kind word to get them through the day. Being kind is learning to step into the shoes of others. It is learning the power of empathy and using it.

Is there a child who needs a pair of shoes? A family who needs food? Someone who needs a place to sleep for just a few days? A lonely, pregnant teenager, that needs someone to talk to? Kindness comes in many forms.

Kindness to others is volunteering at your local homeless shelter or at a pantry that feeds hungry people. Kindness is holding the hand of someone dying of AIDS or cancer. Kindness is letters or visits to those shut in at hospitals or prisons. Kindness is a smile that may pull someone through their day. Kindness is a bag of clothes or toys on the curb, with a sign that reads, *free.*

Do not mistake being a grouch with not having a kind soul. Kindness to others does not mean having to be nice to everyone we meet; ideally it would be wonderful if we could, but that is not the way of the world.

Being kind means not judging others. Drug addicts, ex-cons, homeless, or the mentally ill, most of these people have the potential for kindness and love; they want the same things from life that you do; they have just made a wrong turn on the road of life. Look at them as people, writing their own stories, with the same series of adventures and tears that your own story has.

These people were not born drug addicts or homeless, they had a life that at some point went wrong. No one deserves to be punished for a life gone wrong. Remember, *those you pass going up, are those you pass coming down.* No one is beyond stumbling to the bottom and no one is beyond climbing to the top.

Keep in mind this old proverb as you attempt to help others. *Give a man a fish and he will eat today. Teach a man to fish and he will eat everyday.* The greatest gift you can give a person who has lost his way or who is less fortunate than yourself is the gift knowledge. Give them a gift that will last a life time, teach them how to achieve exactly what you are striving for, happiness and success. Give them power over their lives.

A final word, judge not and be not judged. I find that when people are asking for money they always have a story to tell. "I ran out of gas." "My husband left and the baby needs diapers." "We're collecting for a funeral." These people do not owe anyone an explanation; if you are going to give, then give, and that's the end of it.

An old Rabbi once said. "It is better to give to a hundred men, though only one may be real, then to refuse a hundred men for fear that one might be a fake."

Giving to others and kindness are a team. These are values that you should be proud to hand down to your children, grandchildren, nieces, and nephews. These values must be shown, as opposed to telling for your children to truly understand them.

You want your children to learn honesty, hard work, and responsibility; these are values that they will learn in the process of helping others.

Children must live values. Children must learn at a very early age the value of other human beings. Everyone is not rich or pretty. Not all people do nice things. Other people are writing their own stories and some of those stories may not be very nice, but they are still human beings. You do not want your children to judge others when they do not know the story of that person's life. Teach them sensitivity.

Learning to respect other human beings for whom they are does not mean agreeing with certain life styles. Understanding the nature of being human is a process that some people never learn. Wouldn't it be nice if it started with our children, the future of our world?

You are probably asking yourself, "How can I be a spiritual person? I curse too much, yell too much, and argue with my neighbors and family members. How is it possible for me to be a spiritual person?"

The answer is, you can be, and probably already are. Who cares about a few personality flaws. The guy standing on the corner appreciates you. The lonely kid who was thinking about suicide appreciates you. The family whose son was injured in a car accident appreciates you. The single mother appreciates you. You have probably done more good than you realize. Don't worry about your habits. Don't judge yourself. You are on a journey and you haven't arrived yet; you may never arrive. But, think of all the people you will help along the way, and those you have already helped. You have felt the hardships of life, you have felt pain, loneliness, despair, and anger, and so have the potential to understand others and what they are feeling and experiencing.

You may think you're doing bad or feel that you haven't gotten as much out of life as you expected; but you have more than you can imagine. You possess all of the natural wonders of the world, the beach, the mountains, rivers and lakes. You have things no one else has, your unique life story, your children, your family, friends, and your spouse. Open your mind to what you have and enjoy those gifts.

When you have given your children the ability to appreciate these gifts, and the understanding of other human beings, then they will someday go into the world and pass these gifts on to others. Think of yourself as a teacher who will someday send your tiny vessel into the world bearing gifts to others. Now, how can you say you have nothing? You have power!

Think of all the material things you possess. Do you have a car, a house, a job, a full tank of gas? If you are homeless you can still count what material things you have. Do you have a special corner where you sleep every night, blankets, a basket? Everyone has something; add it up. What about qualities that make you special. Are you filled with drive and faith? Are you healthy? Think of people who have no drive in life, no faith, no hope for the future. These are the tools that give you the power to move forward in life.

Do you have eyes and a mouth? Do you have strong legs that move you where you want to go? These are gifts. If you don't have the gift of sight do you have ears? No one goes without.

Everyone has the gifts they need to move ahead in life, but not everyone is aware of it. You have so much, become aware of it.

Not everyone has all of the same things. You may have a handicap or have experienced such a great loss in your life that you are immobilized. Every life is totally complete, but never totally perfect. It is up to you to find out what you have, and then learn to appreciate and use it to your advantage.

Dreams are part of our spiritual growth. Nothing was ever done that didn't start out as a dream. So dream big and give those dreams life.

You live in a material world. You want and desire material wealth. You have a right to have all the material things you could ever want. But, remember your spiritual world. Remember your spiritual growth. In the spiritual world there is no rich or poor, pretty or ugly. Appreciate your spiritual world as much as your material world. Both combine together to give you everything you will ever need to live your life to the fullest.

Part Three

It's All About Family

✦

Chapter 17

Our Children

✦

Some of you reading this book have children. Some are planning children in the future. And, others are planning to never have children.

If you already have children then you know what wonderful possibilities live in your home. You have experienced the joys, as well as the heartaches, of loving another person so deeply and so intently that your own life takes second place to this natural wonder.

If you are planning to have children in the near or far future, you are going to someday embark on a wonderful, exciting, and sometimes overwhelming journey; different from all others you will ever travel again.

If you choose to not have children, ever, then that is a choice, your choice; and what you choose in life is what works for you. There are wondrous miracles and travels waiting for you to experience and enjoy alone or with a special someone. Children do not define our lives. They are wonderful, but for those who choose to have them.

This chapter will appeal to those who either have or will someday have children. For those of you who choose to be child free, read on anyway, you may have nieces, nephews, or others close to you who are children.

Your goal is to be a good parent, while living a life that is full, happy, resourceful, and successful; this seemingly unreachable task can be done. Your children are not your life; they are a part of your life. Your life has hundreds of branches going in many different directions, each branch is unique, some stronger than others.

With children, come a whole new world of possibilities and responsibilities. Children will color our lives like nothing else can, but they can also, at times, be overwhelming. Children can be hardheaded, spoiled, stubborn, mean, mouthy, ungrateful, messy, irresponsible, loud, destructive, unruly, and rebellious. They can also be, loving, sweet, charming, helpful, inspiring, innocent, imaginative, entertaining, enlightening, fun, positive, and open. So children can, and will, strike a balance in you.

Children depend on you for love, support, safety, and security. These become your responsibilities when you decide to have children. Sometimes, when you have children, it is very hard to stay in touch with your own dreams and goals, because children do zap a good portion of your time and energy. Here's where it gets sticky.

When you have children, you have to become selfish. You have to think about *you* first. If you are not happy; your children are not happy. If you are stressed; your children are stressed. If you are physically drained; your children may feel frightened. If you are sick; your children may feel alone. Your children depend on and trust you. In order to be an effective parent, you have to take care of *you*.

Raising children should be rewarding; it should never be a chore or a burden. Just as you choose to have children, you should also choose to be happy and fulfilled as the parent or guardian of those children. Raising children doesn't just happen, it takes planning, goals, and lots of hard work.

Help children plan their own goals, both for themselves and for the happiness of the family. Show children how wonderful life can be. Teach them about all of the options open to them, about making choices, and about blessings. Give them values that will not only carry them through life, but will leave marks on the lives of others as they pass through.

As you raise your children, you will quickly learn that others might not agree with your ideas, your child rearing techniques, or your family dynamics. In today's society the traditional mother, father, and two point five children no longer exist. Families today are diverse, exciting, and new. And so people will talk, point fingers, and judge these new and dynamic relationships.

Gay parents are ineffective. Children from one-parent families are unsupervised and run wild. Discipline is lax or non-existent in homes headed by aging grandparents. Foster homes are full of delinquents. I'm sure you've heard them all. The time has come for everyone to realize that all families can be successful. And, in every house where there is love, there is a real family.

Here is a story I really like: There was once a farmer coming home from the market riding on an old donkey, his goods securely attached. He met several farmers who angrily accused him of being thoughtless and cruel for making his poor old donkey carry his weight as well as the weight of his goods. Feeling guilty, the farmer got off the donkey. He then continued his journey pulling the old donkey behind him. Along came another group of farmers who laughed at him. How foolish he was to walk, while the donkey carried only the goods, he had a perfectly good donkey that could carry both him and his goods.

The moral of the story is obvious; you will never please everyone no matter how hard you try. So don't waste valuable time trying to please others, it will only zap you of the energy you need for yourself and for those you love.

Raising children takes an abundance of energy, love, and tolerance. And, you will experience an abundance of guilt; you must be willing to toss guilt out the window.

There is no right or wrong way to raise children. You do what you are able to do, give what you have to give, and then move forward. Yes, you are going to make mistakes and even bad choices; but you will survive and your children will survive.

You will never be a perfect parent, but you can always be a good parent. And being a good parent does not mean not making mistakes. You will yell at your kids, and sometimes not like them, and that is okay. Your goal is not perfection. Your goal is to raise your children in a loving and safe environment. Your goal is to raise children who will someday be a blessing to others as they take their place in society.

When you feel like giving up, when you don't like your children, when your life is boring and unproductive, then it's time to stop! A warning is staring you straight in the face. Think of it as a fever, something that is useful, but a warning that something is wrong. Now is the time to evaluate the problem. The lives of your children are entwined in your own, so you will have to examine your entire family dynamics in order to define what the problem may be. Every person in the family is a part of the problem, and every person in the family should be a part of the solution. Take your time and really try to understand what is going on within the walls of your home. Your goal should be to restore balance back into the family unit.

You will pull from all the tools available to you. Those tools can include anything you can imagine; Family group, outside family therapy, individual therapy, parenting classes, books, family, and friends who are familiar with you and your family. Take time to pull as many tools as you can think of and then choose the ones that will benefit your family.

Children are a challenge; some children are more of a challenge than others. But, happily, you have an abundance of options and choices. How will you deal with each child and with each unique situation that pops up? Tap into your options and choices. Not sure what they are? Then grab a pen and a sheet of paper, because now is the time to write down all sorts of ideas. Some will seem silly or inappropriate, don't worry, you can eliminate later. Right now just get all of your ideas out. Slowly, start incorporating those ideas into your daily life with your children. Move slow and watch as the positive changes begin to form in your life and in the life of your family.

Guilt is obsolete; throw it away. You are doing the best you can do and that is enough when there is an abundance of love.

Chapter 18

Life Situations

✦

There are going to be acute situations that pop up in your life; events that happen suddenly, without warning. Do not view these events as disruptive, life shattering, obstacles in your life. Look at these events as experiences and challenges that will empower you during difficult times. You have not come to a red light in life; you have come to a yellow light, with time to plan and think before you act. There are no wrong choices. Choices can be changed. Experiment with all of the choices available to you and even play with some crazy ideas. Decide what will work best for you, then do it.

Life is fluid, so that makes every idea and choice a go. We have a freeway where I live that is a nightmare at the interchange. People wait for long periods of time to even enter the ramp. I don't. I drive right past car after car, and at the entrance to the ramp I slip in (I know what you're thinking; it is an irritating maneuver to other drivers.) Now, the reason I can do this is because I know another route that is just as good. So if for some reason I can't get in, I just continue to the other route. This gives me the freedom to move past the long line of cars, because I know I can't make a wrong choice, no matter what, I am still on track.

And that, my friend, is how life is. You make a choice and if it isn't the right choice then you have the freedom to make another choice. Do not get caught up in what you did wrong. If one choice doesn't work for you, another choice will. Each choice you make is nothing more than an adventure, and with every adventure comes risk. *Take the risk!* All you need is faith. You have the freedom to set some really exciting goals and plans for your life.

There is no blueprint for dealing with acute situations that pop up in your life such as job or home loss, or a family death or illness, they happen too suddenly and unexpectedly. Acute situations hit most of us like a brick wall and rarely are we prepared for the event. Your initial reactions and choices may be made at an emotional level, until you have had time to think the situation through. When an acute situation strikes you may not have time to plan and may have to resort to quick fix choices. Do what you have to do to get things in balance, even for just the moment. Then, before you do anything else, **stop,** until you feel like you have some control over your thoughts and your emotions. Take as long as you need to pull yourself together and evaluate the situation. Life is a hands' on adventure and acute situations can be a powerful learning experience.

First and foremost, don't panic! Take a deep breath and when you are ready make some quick choices. Your choices will be a temporary fix for the problem, until you have had time to come up with a permanent plan or solution. If you already know what you have to do to get things back on track, then do it. If you slip into panic mode (and that can easily happen) you are not using your faith. Stop and allow your faith to take over. A few moments in meditation, before acting, should get you into quick touch with your faith. In acute situations you are always going to need your faith.

Then there are those chronic events; situations that seem to go on and on. These may include ongoing feelings of frustration, anger, fear, family problems, money issues, or conflicts at work. The list is endless. I guarantee you that everyone has at least one chronic issue going on in their lives. Chronic situations will force you to depend on your faith and actively seek out coping skills.

Start by taking time out to analyze the situation. There is a possibility that you can learn to live with the problem, after a few minor changes. Or maybe, it is a problem that has to be changed. Think about the problem, who it involves, and the impact it is having on your life. If possible write everything down on a sheet of paper.

Time out not only gives you a chance to evaluate your situation, but you should also use this time to formulate a plan of action. Have several plans, then choose the ones you feel will work the best for you. Put your faith to work and begin to carry out your plans without fear of change. Add patience, because you know nothing is going to change this very second. Last, persevere. Stick to your choices and give them a chance to work. Know that things are going to happen. Don't give in to soon.

What are you willing to do to change a bad situation? You may be dealing with spousal problems, money issues, a child out of control, it doesn't matter what the problem is. All problems require the same initial mode of action.

- *Evaluate the problem.*
- *Look at your options*
- *Make choices*
- *Plan/ set goals.*
- *Put your plans into action*

What you decide to do will depend on you, your feelings, what you want and need to move on in life, and the amount of risk you are willing to take.

Examine your feelings. What will make you happy? Explore why this child's behavior upsets you. How extensive are your money problems? How bad is the situation at work or at home? How much of an impact does this problem have on your life? To what extent is the family unit being affected? What ever the problem is, exploration of your feelings is a positive starting point.

If you take the time to really study your feelings, you may come up with some shocking revelations about yourself. You may decide that certain behaviors of your spouse, children, or co-workers, can be lived with, if you are willing to change the way you are looking at the situation. Explore your problem with an open mind. (And I say your problem, because it is your problem.) You are changing your thoughts, your feelings, and your ideas about what the problem is. It's all about you, because what affects you may not even bother another person. Remember, every problem belongs to the person who owns it.

The problem isn't that your child is always mouthing off; the problem may really be that your child's attitude upsets you. Your child may not think he has a smart mouth at all. The problem isn't that you are behind in your bills and your husband spends too much money; the problem may really be that you have no spending plan and money is always tight. Your husband may have no idea that he is spending too much money. So, as you can see, you have to define the problem in relation to how it is affecting you, how it makes you feel, and to what extent you are willing to learn to live with the problem or change it. Your goal is not to change anyone else; your goal is to change your own thoughts and beliefs in order to mold the problem into something you can live with.

And remember, nothing is trivial or silly. If something bothers you then you have the right to change it. There are hundreds of choices and ways of dealing with every situation; one of them will work for you. It all boils down to what is most comfortable for you, how much risk you are willing to take, what changes you are willing to make, and what will make you happy and bring harmony back into your life.

Ask yourself questions such as, can I live with this situation? What am I willing to do to make changes? What am I willing to give up? How bad is the situation? How much worse can it get? What will make me happy? There are tons of questions and it is your job to ask every one of them. Remember, you are doing this for you, to reduce your level of stress and replace the balance in your life. Conflicts in relationships, money issues, and depression, all take from precious time that you should be enjoying your life.

Pull together all of your resources: faith, perseverance, patience. Other resources may include friends, family, books, and classes. Every tool you can think of can be used. Do what ever is easy and comfortable for you. Don't stress about resources, allow them to happen naturally.

Resources include all of the plans and goals you have already made. All of the questions you have asked yourself and others, all of your feelings that you have explored. There is no limit to your resources.

Wake up and look at all the positives in your life. Everyday you are given another morning, another day, another chance at life. Everyday can end with the words, "it was such a good, productive, and happy day." Everyday can end with thoughts of fulfillment, peace, contentment, and feelings of success. Everyday, you can move one more step toward your goals, your dreams, and your life.

Look over your goals for each new day. Look at any problems you may have had the day before and acknowledge that something went wrong; weather it was your fault or not. Focus on both the positive and negative events that happened and how you could have handled the situation differently or how you handled it right.

The goal is not to stress over a past event, the goal is to close each day in a positive way. Maybe you had an argument with your daughter or you may have felt overwhelmed for some reason. Go over those problems and give them some sort of closure or put them on your things to work on list. Don't make a big deal of it; but do be aware of the events of each day.

Take time to review your future goals, do this when things are quite and you have a few extra minutes. Make sure your goals are still consistent with your current needs and dreams. Remember that each new day is a gift; what you do with that gift is your choice.

Chapter 19

Appreciation Of Life And Family

✦

The beginning of any journey has to start with you, the traveler, feeling good about yourself. Every dream and every goal is waiting to be pursued. But, before you begin your journey, stop and think about how blessed you are and how much you deserve everything you have already achieved. It is not just about being blessed; it is about knowing how blessed you are.

Look around you and start to see how much you already have. You have so much more than just material wealth; you have the entire world. The world is the greatest gift of all to you and to your loved ones. Majestic mountains, caterpillars, roly-poly bugs, lakes, rivers, streams, dirt, rain, sunshine, its all yours and its all free.

Everything is here for you, but you have to be willing to take it. Take a hike with the kids or alone. Delight in the discovery of a small stream babbling down a hill, a patch of wild flowers or a snow capped mountain. Watch and discover how ants live, work, and play. Bestow upon your children a love of learning, the most valuable gift you can offer them.

Give your children, nieces, nephews, and grandchildren the world as a classroom and watch them blossom. Teach them to respect the elusive gift of time and to freely use their gift of choice. Give them a love of nature and all it has to offer.

What is the worst scenario? You have no car and no money to get to all of these wonderful places where nature is abundant. No excuse! Take a walk around your own backyard and discover the treasures there. There are trees to climb and bugs to hold. Pull up a handful of weeds or flowers and let your children study the roots. Go to the library and travel the world. Discover and learn about the world that begins in your own back yard.

Take a bus to the beach. There is a special peace that crawls over you when you are sitting on the beach. The sound of the waves, birds swooping across the white sand, your children happily at play, this is true bliss. Do not allow your life to become nothing more than work, bills, and unfulfilled dreams.

Plan a camping trip and get away in the summer. No time? Then do it once a year, but do it. Hate camping? Then plan another outing, something more suited to the personalities of your own family. Talk about all the possibilities available to you with your family and then decide on a trip with a budget that you can live with. That budget may be as low as twenty dollars, but even twenty dollars is a potential adventure. Now you have taken the first step. If you are beginning to organize your life and your faith is becoming stronger, you should have no trouble finding the time to enjoy your world.

People, who get more, are those who take more. This is something you should say out loud, think about, and then apply to your life. *People, who get more, are those who take more.* Every goal you set, every dream you dream, every want and need you have, is within your grasp. Take from the world all that is offered to you. Take the gifts that flow through your life. Learn to recognize when the answers to your wants and needs have come.

Learn to appreciate the world you live in. Learn to appreciate the gifts your children, spouse, and family members bring into your life and how this has enriched your very existence.

Realize how blessed you are to have so much. This is what life is all about, having so much and learning to appreciate and enjoy all of it. And you are even more blessed to have choices of how you will spend your time enjoying all of your gifts.

Life is exciting and having family and friends to enjoy it with is a gift unsurpassed by all others. Take a walk, jog, hike, go outside and watch the sunset, or meditate. One gift to yourself is a gift to all of those around you. When you are swimming in joy, all of those close to you will share in the joy that you are experiencing. They will feel at peace with themselves, because you are at peace with yourself. When you are happy, your children are happy. When you are filled with positive energy, your friends are filled with the same positive energy that you pass on to them. When you are at your best, your spouse is at his or her best. When you are stress free, those around you are stress free. The gifts between you, your children, your friends, and your family, have no ending. Positive energy forms a positive circle, and it extends to those in the circle, and even to those outside of the circle.

Every day brings new experiences and new opportunities. Time is a precious commodity, use what you have wisely. Using your time wisely can be very subjective; it can mean anything from falling asleep under the stars, to an exotic trip to another country, and everything in between. What is here today will be here tomorrow. There is no perfect time. Anytime is the perfect time. Time is precious, valuable, and always here. How you choose to use your time is your choice. How you choose to use the gifts life has given to you is your choice. If you choose to use your time sleeping, drugged out, locked away from the world, drowning in depression, hating and hurting others, or whining about how unfair life is, that is your choice. You have *gifts, choices*, and *time* (although your time is very limited.) Put the three together and use them to open your world or use them to find reasons to complain about life.

Some people travel through life and never use any of their gifts. They allow random events to make all of their choices. Their time is wasted on empty days, loneliness, and unbearable hours. This is their choice. Then, there are others who squeeze every minute out of a day, even if it is just planning goals in the last minutes before they fall asleep.

Life is an adventure and the excitement of where you are going is a part of that adventure. Your travels will be full of choices that can be changed from minute to minute, day to day, and year to year. Plan, dream, and act; don't worry about wrong choices because choices can be changed to reflect new goals, dreams, and desires. Use your time in ways that will enhance your life. Make choices that will give you the best return on your time and gifts.

How will your children utilize what they have been given? How will you utilize what you have been given?

Chapter 20

Communication

✦

We communicate everyday, at work, at home, with our kids, our friends, our enemies, and even with our pets. Let's look at communication in our everyday lives, how it can help or hinder us, and how we can use less of it and still get by. Let's begin by understanding communication and how we utilize it in our everyday lives.

We communicate with others in three ways; we talk *to them, with them* or *at them*. Most people utilize all three when communicating depending on whom they are talking to and the circumstances.

Communication is basic to every relationship in life. Communication should be open and honest with everyone you meet and especially with those closest to you. Of course, open and honest doesn't mean telling your neighbor she is fat or giving away family secrets just because someone asked for some juicy information. The words, open and honest, means using your ability to communicate to enhance your relationships with others, such as when giving valuable information to your children or students.

Talking to others involves communicating basic ideas such as the rules in your home, job duties or about life in general. Talking to others is basic; you use plenty of it, at home and at work. When you talk to your children, friends or co-workers you communicate your values, ideas, dreams, and expectations. Talking helps us to grow and learn.

This level of communication is valuable and healthy. There is no judging or put downs, there is only ideas, facts, and knowledge being passed from one person to another.

Talking with someone is your everyday chit-chat. When you talk with your children, friends, family, lovers or co-workers you want and benefit from the information they pass to you. They, in return, appreciate the feedback you give to them. When people talk with each other everyone feels important and equal in their ideas, feelings, beliefs and thoughts. Talking with others is a special time when you pass on your feelings about things that are important to you. And (depending on the relationship) you confide in each other about secret things. We all need to make time for this kind of meaningful communication between ourselves and others.

When you have children talking with them can build and strengthen your relationship. You can talk with your child while driving to the store, school, or to grandma's house. You can talk while you are cooking or doing dishes. In other words, you do not have to find a special block of time when you are sitting and giving one hundred percent of your attention to your child. Talking with your children is one of the times when you are their friend and not just their parent. All ages benefit and enjoy being talked with, from the smallest toddler to the grown adult. When you talk with someone it usually just happens, it is not something you can set up in a schedule.

Talking at someone is your everyday ranting and raving. It can turn into a screaming match between people. Usually when you are talking at someone, no one is listening, no one is respecting the other, and no one has any desire to hear the other side. It is human to get mad at others and say things that are not very nice. Talking at others is not always good or beneficial, but human. Talking at others is never an effective means of communication. Most of us resort to this form of communication when we are stressed or just too tired and rushed to care.

Many of us probably talk at our children, a lot. We get irritated at our children and can (during a complete melt down) yell at them about everything they ever did from the moment they were born. The important point to remember is that when you do yell at your kids, and you will, don't spend unnecessary time after the incident feeling guilty. What is done is done; you are not a bad or abusive parent, you are human. Move on now. Tell your children you're sorry (if you are.) Be aware of what sparked the outburst and how you could have handled it differently. Use the incident as a learning experience. Dwelling on a screeching, yelling, out-of-control episode won't change it and chances are the kid's have already forgotten about it anyway. You won't stop yelling after one incident, but as you become more aware of your yelling episodes the incidents will be reduced in number, and every step forward is good.

When talking at someone, for what ever reason, acknowledge your anger, understand it, and learn to control it. So, your fate isn't sealed, you are not a monster. Move on. If you feel you can't control the angry days and anger dominates your relationships with everyone around you, then seek help. Asking for help is a part of knowing that there are alternatives open to you. You are not alone. Help and support is there for you, if you choose to seek it out and use it.

Talking at others is never productive for anyone. You do let off built up hurt and anger and sometimes this can be good. Anger can be positive if you are learning from it. Your goal should be the ability to talk to or with others, not at them.

Communication within an intimate relationship is crucial to the relationship. If there were only one ingredient to the success of a relationship, communication would be my choice (you can disagree with this). Communication keeps you open to the needs and desires of each other.

Communication is something we will use every single day of our lives. It can be positive or negative, productive or wasteful. Learning to communicate effectively is important. It will determine how our relationships will blossom or die. Communication skills give us power, but can also make us appear weak and ineffective. Become aware of your communication skills and how you present yourself, not only to your children, but to others as well.

I find using fewer words always works best. Get your ideas and beliefs across in as few words as possible. Long conversations, scolding and lectures, are nothing more than a string of words, and more then likely the other person has stopped listening.

Choose your words and make every word important and worth listening to.

Communicate with others in a positive and meaningful way. The tongue is the window to the heart. Be careful how you use words. Words can stab like a knife, burn like fire, and leave unseen scars in the hearts of others.

Chapter 21

Significant Others

✦

Everyone needs a support system. Support systems are people who are there for you when you need them. A significant other or support system can be your husband, wife, boyfriend, girlfriend, parent, grandparent, teacher, even your ex-spouse. Anyone who supports and understands you is a potential support system. There are also social support systems, such as groups, counselors, or therapists that you can tap into.

The extended family should be your strongest support system and for many people it is. But, for others, this loving system is not available. For our purposes let's define the extended family to include parents, grandparents, siblings, cousins, aunts and uncles. This would include adopted family members, stepparents, step-grandparents and stepchildren. It would also include all foster children.

Most of us are so busy in the course of a day that we tend to alienate ourselves. We are so busy with work, family, and all the other obligations we are faced with everyday, that we have little time for romance or for keeping friendships alive. As a result we end up alone and we turn inward. We might begin to feel unloved, unappreciated, and scared. Now is the time to reach out.

As human beings we tend to naturally be sociable. To satisfy this natural part of our human nature we have been blessed with family, friends and lovers. These people are crucial to your well being both physically and mentally.

The many relationships you form in your life become a part of the fabric of your life. A vast and diverse fabric will give you a sense of emotional security.

That's not to say you have to hang out with family and friends all the time to receive the benefits. You do need to be aware that they are available and probably happy to be there for you when you need help, even if you just need someone to talk to. And the coin is two sided, you have an obligation to be there for them, as well.

I am not talking about the person who is an emotional sponge, who soaks in every ounce of energy you have. These people deserve your respect, but they have far greater needs then you can possibly be expected to deal with. Encourage these people to seek out other resources available to meet their needs.

If you find yourself involved in an unhealthy relationship, consider seeking professional help or confide in another person who knows your situation. Your goal is not only a life that is productive and stress free, but also happy and healthy. An emotionally draining relationship or an abusive relationship is not the solution.

You will not jump out of an unhealthy relationship just by reading this book, but you will become aware of it and can begin to gain the strength you are going to need to change your situation; if you choose to do that.

A relationship should be a positive experience. It is very difficult to escape from an unhealthy relationship. The person in an abusive relationship has a life that is probably very overwhelming and out of control. An abuser has the uncanny ability to give the abused person just what they think they want or need.

You often hear this coming from insensitive or uninformed people. "She must like it or she would leave him." Sure, that's easy to say. These people have no idea of the emotional dynamics of this relationship. They have no idea of the pain, fear, and mixed feelings the abused person might be feeling. It is not easy to get out of an unhealthy or abusive relationship, but wanting to make a change and being aware that something in not right is a good healthy start.

Begin with your faith and move slowly from there. Don't just assume that you are going to get up one day and say, "that's it!" and walk out. For some men or women this is possible, but for most of us it will take a little more work. If you have already acknowledged the fact that you are in an unhealthy situation, then you have taken the first step. Baby steps, tiny moves forward, these are all a start in the right direction and all you might be able to do right now; and that's okay.

Have faith and take tiny steps, such as a phone call to a friend or an appointment with a therapist. No one can tell you how much you should do or what you should do as you define the relationship you are in, and decide if this is the relationship you want; others can only suggest, the rest is up to you. Think and act slow and with purpose.

Many people who are abused and mistreated in a relationship have bruised and sensitive self esteems. This puts them at a disadvantage and makes them easy pray for the abuser.

Let's take a closer look at the different relationships we form in our lives and how they can help or hurt us.

Husbands, Wives And Lovers

Most everyone will at some time in their life become attached to another. This intimate attachment will lead to marriage or some other type of similar relationship.

Your spouse will become your other half. You will become as one, but will remain separate. Your goals and dreams will live on and hopefully blossom with the help of your other half. And that's how this type of union should be, one of complete love and deep commitment to each other. The perfect union would be one in which each partner allows the other to dream and plan goals that have the power to take shape and grow. You are team mates.

Of course no relationship is truly made in heaven and there will be conflicts, usually brought on by a lack of communication. Each of you will be right half of the time. You would not want to be right all of the time. By admitting you are wrong sometimes, gives you the opportunity to grow and learn from the wisdom of your partner. Learn from each other, it is one of the benefits of the relationship.

Not everyone will agree with your relationship. Aside from abuse, there is no one who should tell you to leave your spouse or tell you what type of relationship you should have. Others do not really know what is going on in your relationship. No matter how much you tell friends and family or how much others confide in you about their relationship, there is always more. So only you (and your spouse) can decide where your relationship is headed.

Don't allow others to make you feel guilty if you choose to stay in a relationship that *they* think is bad; you be the judge of what is good or bad in your relationship.

The goal of any relationship is to foster each others dreams and goals, and to give each other support while moving through life. Make a list of what goals you have for your own unique relationship and talk to your spouse. Communication is the number one ingredient of a successful relationship. Together, you and your spouse should talk about what each of you desire in your relationship and pull together ideas that will make your union as dynamic as it can possibly be.

Relationships have the power to bring out the best in each person. Relationships can also destroy a person; holding them down and ripping their goals and dreams to shreds. Look at your relationship and see where you are at and where you want to be then, make the choices that will benefit you and take you in the direction you want to go.

Life should be happy and exciting, an adventure that you are thrilled to face each day; not something that tears the life out of you, until you can barely crawl out of bed. Where is your relationship at right now? Take the time to evaluate your relationship. The union of marriage is the most intimate you will form in your life; don't downplay its importance or the impact it will have on your future, or the future of your children.

No matter where your relationship is, you have the choice to make it better, if both persons are willing to work at it. No relationship can ever be perfect; you will continue to have conflicts. Relationships take work on a daily basis. Eventually, you will strike a balance where you are both willing to give all you have to make the other happy. Make yourself happy too; you are one as a couple, but still two unique persons.

If for some reason you are being held back by an abusive or compromising relationship then take steps to move forward, even if that may mean moving forward alone.

A relationship should not be in a rut or static. Relationships should be exciting, loving, and dynamic, always changing, but always for the best of each other.

Stop periodically and get a tune up on your relationship before you continue your journey. Relationships are unique. Don't compare your relationship to the relationship of others. You are unique and your spouse is unique, together you are a team. Be a winning team; always bring out the best in each other.

Kids

One of your most fulfilling, but most challenging relationships will be your children. That would include any children you share some form of parental relationship with.

Your children will both love and hate you. They will make you proud and embarrass you. They will fill you with both joy and dread. You will worry about them and sometimes wish you didn't have children at all. Your relationship with your children will change from day to day and even from minute to minute. Bottom line is, you love them and they love you.

You and your children are stuck together. You didn't choose each other, your relationship just happened, weather you were brought together by birth, adoption, or some other means. You are blessed. And, children are a blessing from birth to adulthood. This dynamic relationship will change and grow over time. But it will be a relationship that will never end, even if you stop talking to each other, you will continue to have some sort of relationship.

You owe these children. You owe them values and you owe them the understanding of how lucky they are to be living this life. Show them what gifts life has to offer them and then let them choose the path they want to travel. No matter what path they choose, you know that you have given them the knowledge and tools they need to be successful.

Our children are writing their own stories and they will make wrong turns in life. **Don't panic.** Making a wrong turn isn't the end of life, it is only a choice that can be changed, and most kids eventually get on the right road. For every person who made a bad choice in life they have a parent who loves them, just like you love your child, even when they make bad choices. Bad choices and wrong turns do not constitute the end. Life is fluid and can be changed.

Give your child the tools he or she will need to carry them through life. Teach them about dreams and goals. Teach them what values you embrace and allow them to write their own stories.

It is true; there are children who really do not have anyone who love them. And there are others who turn off the road of life and never get back on; these are the ones you have to reach out to when you have the opportunity. You may make a change in the life of another, and one person helped is one less person on the wrong road. For the ones less fortunate, pray for them and know that they have the same options in life that you have. They are writing a story and even from the most horrid of life beginnings people have pulled themselves up.

For the average child, who has parents who love and cherish them, parents who have spent countless hours guiding them and giving them opportunities to expand their world; these children are blessed. Continue to help these children realize their potential and encourage them to seek out their blessings.

Once your children are grown does not signal the end of your life. You have a lot left to do and see and become. Children learn when they see their parents living and enjoying life and that is how it should be. Generation after generation living life, taking all the free gifts the world has to offer, giving to others, facing challenges, and being truly happy and satisfied with all of your choices, goals and dreams.

Life does not stop when the kids move out; it begins all over again with challenges, problems and thrilling adventures unique to where you are at and where you want to go.

The Extended Family

The extended family is a wonderful support system available to you. Lucky is the family who can gather for holidays and family functions, and who can share in each others joys and sorrows. Not everyone has this large extended family, and that is okay. We manage with what we have and we learn to appreciate our own positions in life.

For those who do have family, embrace this extended unit. The size of a family doesn't matter, what matters is the shared love and respect family members have for each other, and yes, even the drama.

You may not have an extended family that you were born or adopted into, but were you blessed enough to join another extended family, maybe through your spouse or a friend, one that truly embraces you as one of their own? Then you have an extended family.

Some of you have family members such as a sibling, parent, or a cousin, you haven't spoke to in years; maybe there was an argument or an issue that couldn't be resolved at the time. If this is the case, ask yourself how important it is for you to have this person back in your life. Maybe it's not important at all, and that's okay. But if having this family member back in your life is something you want to happen, then it is time to act.

There is no good or bad time to make something happen, there is only now. Now is the time to act. Decide how you want to approach this family member. Maybe writing a letter is easier for you than talking to them in person. Do what is easiest and most comfortable for you. There is the chance that this person may not respond to you in a positive way; be prepared for this. Don't let your pride get in the way of what you want to accomplish.

There is a Jewish holiday called Yom Kippur, this holiday is a time to ask for forgiveness from those we have hurt and to forgive those who have hurt us. It goes as far as to say we should approach this person three times. So approach this person and either ask for forgiveness or forgive them for what ever it is they have done to you. To forgive is cleansing. No matter what the outcome, you will feel lighter within yourself.

The extended family can be a positive force in your life. Reach out to make and keep your family unit strong.

Friends

Of course, we all know how positive and healthy it is to have friends. Some people have an abundance of friends and others have only one or two. Having friends is a benefit of life that has its own healing powers. You need friends, at least one who you can depend on and who can depend on you.

What is a friend? A friend is what ever you believe a friend to be. For me a friend is someone you can be yourself with, someone who accepts you with all of your faults, someone you enjoy being with and who enjoys being with you. You have things in common with a friend and enjoy sharing a two-way relationship. A friend is someone whose needs are being met just by your presence and vice versa. Friendship forms a balance between needs and wants. Friends are there for you. You both may be experiencing a full and hectic life, as well as deep emotional issues, but you will still be able to strike a balance between a fair give and take. That is what makes a friendship work.

How do you nurture and keep a real friendship alive? That is as individual as the question. For one person nurturing a friendship may be to spend time together, weather chit chatting on the phone or going to the mall together. For another person it may be the security of knowing that your friend will always be there for you, even if you rarely see each other. In hard times you can give a friend a call and they'll spring into action, just as you would do for them. Being friends doesn't have to mean constantly being together. Best friends sometimes live miles apart and rarely see each other, but they are always there for each other.

Some friends only need time together once a year to nourish themselves, such as friends who live in different states and visit once or twice a year. Then there are always the friends whom you never forget to send cards to at Christmas or invite to your daughters wedding. You know these friends are there, even if you never see them. Friendships need to be nurtured and it is up to you to decide how you will do that. We relate differently to different friends. How we achieve this bond with each friend can be a positive experience for them and for us.

If you don't have at least one friend, then keep your eyes and heart open to the possibilities. Maybe you have a co-worker who you really like. There might be someone at the various places you go regularly such as the health spa, a playgroup, the grocery store. Don't force yourself, but do become aware of your need for a friend, someone who will be there for you. Be open-minded. Your friend could be male or female, a handicapped person, or a gay person. Don't limit yourself to someone who appears to be just like you, because what is on the outside may be different from the inside. Be open and play with it.

Having a friend will to some extent cut into your valuable time and limited emotional resources, but the pay off will be priceless. Don't force yourself to give more than you are able. When the right person comes alone you will magically find time to pursue the relationship.

The goal is a support system. You must be willing to give to the relationship. And, most important you must be willing to take what your friend has to offer, without guilt.

Acquaintances

The largest groups of people you will come in contact with are your everyday acquaintances. Weather you like or dislike them; they play a role in your life. Acquaintances benefit us, even if it is just to teach us a lesson about some aspect of life. Every person you pass as you travel through life has something to offer to you, if you are willing to open yourself to the possibilities.

The bum in the street becomes an acquaintance if you are touched by him in some way. An acquaintance can be a co-worker, someone you see daily, but do no more then say hi to. Store clerks, the mailman, the school bus driver. You might have an acquaintance who you have a sour relationship with, such as a nasty tempered neighbor. An acquaintance is someone you pass in the streets or it could be someone you have known for years but never bothered to talk to. All of these people have the potential to teach you something or give something to you. Become aware and alert to these unknowns.

Some of these people will pass through your life like a whisper in the wind and you may not even know they exist; become aware of what they might have left behind. Open yourself to how much acquaintances might affect your life and use this knowledge to better your life in some way. Become aware of all the acquaintances you pass every day. Who are they? What do they look like? What do they do? How are they connected to you? How have they affected your life, even in the tiniest way?

Lessons can be learned from every person that crosses your path. A mean, nasty tempered person could teach you to assert yourself or how to deal with stressful situations. Homeless and beggars teach humanity and to appreciate what you have. Children that pass through your life can teach you the meaning of being free and open to life. Co-workers can teach you how to get along with others and about fairness. The lady in the grocery store can teach you the differences in other people. Many lessons are to be learned from every person that comes into and passes through your life. Become aware of the lessons others are offering you with their presence; and become aware of what you might, unknowingly, be giving to them.

Become aware of the people and the energy that surrounds you. While standing in line at the bank, at the grocery store or at the doctor's office, stop and allow the energy that surrounds you to become a part of your life. Every person that passes through your life, even for a brief second, has a lesson to offer. What does a beautiful smile say when you are having a bad day? What are those children saying as they run around the waiting room? Open yourself; you have nothing to lose and much to gain.

And, of course, some of your acquaintances will become your friends. These are friendships that have a beautiful and unexpected start. We are by nature social creatures. Even the most shy of us has a basic need to be social with others. Take advantage of your social nature and tap into your vast resources of acquaintances.

Remember, if you are too tired to even think about these people as they move through your life, then that's okay, it won't change the course of your life, *or will it?*

Negative People, Positive People

As we journey through life we are going to come in contact with hundreds and thousands of people. Most will move through your life and leave only hints of their presence. Some leaving nothing more than good or bad feelings, a thought, an idea, or a new belief, most of these people are positive people with their own lives and their own stories. But you are also going to run into negative people.

You want to steer clear of negative forces. Some people are so down or negative about life that all you can do is give them a kind word or ignore them and move on. It's sad, but negative forces influence your own positive energy.

There will be people who will bring you down, not always because they want to, but because they don't know any better. There are people who will lie and deceive you, thus causing negative things to happen in your life. When this happens you have to get back up and move on. Sometimes, it will be hard to start over, depending on the negative forces that have interfered with your life; but with faith you will.

People may influence you to do things that are illegal or immoral. There are others who are so deeply depressed and negative about life that you are uncomfortable just being around them. It could be a family member, someone who you can't just walk away from. These negative forces have no place in your life. But being human, these others will touch or influence us in some way. Negative people, can and will, bring you down, but they can also make you stronger. Stay in control. Stay strong.

If you are feeling sad, scared or negative about a situation, or a person, then you have already taken the first step because you sense, or know, something is not right. Take a stand. You have to make a choice of how much you are willing to allow this person to affect you.

Negative people can rob you of time and energy. You have very little of either. Time and energy are valuable resources, not to be wasted. Every person you pass has made choices and they have the same power that you have to change what ever it is in their lives that is holding them back.

Negative people have stories too. Understand this and be slow to judge, but, do not allow negative forces to slow you down. What ever you can do to restore positive energy into the life of another person, do it. You are a vessel passing through the lives of many people, both positive and negative, and you have something positive to share. Give what you can and hope someone will take what you leave, then move on.

Part Four

Making It Work

✦

Chapter 22

Finances

◆

Money, now there's a word that can start your emotional juices flowing. If you have ample money to pay the bills, keep the kids in decent clothes, keep your tank full of gas, drive a car you aren't ashamed to drive, and still have a little left over to blow, then money is going to be emotionally sweet to your senses. On the other hand and more realistic, if you are behind in the bills, the kid's have outgrown their shoes, the bank account as well as the gas tank are empty, and extra cash is a foreign word, then the thought of money is going to be a bitter subject for you.

For our purposes we are going to assume that you have financial issues. Until things start to change (and they will) you are going to learn to live within your current financial situation and use what you have to your advantage. In this chapter, you are going to learn to use your faith in all of your financial matters. You are going to dream of wealth and explore ways of achieving it. I can not tell you how to get rich; I can only motivate you toward the possibility and reality of being rich.

There are definitely ways to gain financial freedom, have your bills paid, and still have enough left over to enjoy the fun things in life. *Money can be manipulated*. Making money, having money, using money, and blowing money, is all part of a game that you play every day. It all has to do with the choices you make and your ability or willingness to risk. At the least you are going to learn to manage your finances to your advantage.

Money can (and does) affect the quality of your life. Money can be stressful, both having and not having it. Many people have limited resources; you must not allow your financial situation to control you. No matter what your financial situation, you can control the money that flows through your hands and into your life. Your money problems are not going to magically disappear, but they can be tamed. Money is not going to magically flow into your hands, but there are ways of making money, if you are willing to risk and believe that financial freedom is possible.

Money has to be put into its proper perspective. Begin by evaluating what role money plays in your life and the emotional bonds it has on you. Does money define who you are? Do you feel worthless and beneath other people who have more? Are you free and wild with money, not caring where it goes? Do you believe those with money are better than those without money? Examine your complete financial situation and your beliefs about money. Look at where you are at financially today, and where you want to be in a year, two years, or five years. Explore what role money will play in your life today and in the future.

Think about ways you can enjoy life today with the money you have and still be able to meet your financial needs, goals, and obligations. Once you have a clear picture of your financial goals and beliefs, you will be ready to begin using your goal setting skills, visualize your financial future and create a plan on how you will get to where you want to be.

This all adds up to simply thinking about your financial goals, writing them down, having faith and believing in yourself, your goals, and your dreams. Writing your goals down should include steps that you will take to achieve those goals. A mental picture of what you want in the future should be a part of your goals. Think about this picture, believe it and write it down. Imagine this picture as though it were already happening. Feel the power and sweetness of your dreams.

Don't put your immediate needs and dreams aside for your future goals; the now works hand-in-hand with the future. You must enjoy life now, at the same time that you are working toward improving your financial future. Don't give up that camping trip or that family vacation to Disney World, enjoying life now is as important as your future goals and happiness. Your goal should not be to give anything up, but to have it all; now *and* in the future. Make choices on what can be enjoyed now (your priorities) and what can be put aside for the future.

Make a list of things that are important to you now and things that can wait for future happiness. Is a family vacation important or a new car, or can they wait until next year? I love vacations, but I have had to put them on hold for other things that took priority, and there are other times when my vacation plans were the priority. This doesn't mean to disregard bills and future goals; it just means to not allow your financial situation to limit your life experiences that you should be enjoying today. Remember tomorrow isn't promised to us, but today is already here.

Juggle your resources, plan, dream, and have faith. Goals, dreams, and faith are what will motivate you forward toward what you want and need now and in the future.

Finances are a major part of our lives weather you are very rich, very poor, or anywhere in-between. You must learn to manage your money. But more important, you must learn to manage your money in such a way that will allow you to live your life today, pay your obligations, and still plan for your future. It isn't an easy job. It will take all the faith, perseverance, and patience you have, but it can be done. *Plan, set goals, dream, and act.*

At first, you will stumble through the complicated world of finances and wonder how you can actually live for the now, pay bills, and still take care of your future. **It can be done**. Financial success will happen on different levels for everyone. Some people are willing to take more risks, others will have a tad more faith, and some people are very conservative, testing the waters before taking the risk. What ever personal style you use toward gaining financial freedom is okay, as long as those goals are planned, set firmly in your mind, and you are taking the necessary steps that will propel you forward.

Don't expect (at first) to go on cruises, travel to exotic destinations, and pay for scuba diving lessons while paying a mountain of bills, and still stashing away for the future on a minimum wage. Be creative, yet realistic. What financial goals are you going to set for today? What financial goals are you going to set for your future?

Your finances are in your hands. Even a meager income has to be managed for you to get the full benefits. Some people have it easier than other's; this is a reality of life. Make plans on the level you are at, set goals, and wait for your financial situation to get better. Most important, *believe it will get better.* Have you ever played the game of monopoly? Financial issues can be a challenging and rewarding game. Think about every move before you make it, challenge yourself; then move forward.

Money and risk go hand-in-hand, don't let that aspect of the game scare you; take the risk. **Without some level of risk there can be no change**. Everyday (for just seconds a day) visualize exactly where you want to be financially. While you are visualizing, believe it is really happening and get really excited about your financial future. You have nowhere to go, but up.

Chapter 23

Money, And What It Means To Me

✦

Money has different meanings to different people. To some, it is an indication of how successful they are in life; these people may live in the biggest houses and drive the finest cars. To others, it means nothing more than something to eat; these people could care less about what others think, they don't have big fancy houses and may drive economical cars or use the city bus. Upward mobility is important to some and means nothing to others. Both of these life choices are okay. It's all about being happy and satisfied with where you are at and where you want to be.

The majority of us fall in the middle; satisfied with where we are financially, but most of us could use just a little more. We are the people who want nice things from life, such as a spacious house, a nice car, nice clothes, (in) toys and gadgets, extra money for after school sports, vacations, and a little extra money in our pockets after the bills are paid.

Is that asking too much?

Religious institutions teach that money is the root of all evil. *Maybe,* What do you think? Do you believe that money is the root of all evil? Or do you believe that money is a gift, a blessing that makes our lives easier and opens us to greater possibilities?

Is money something you can pray for and get? Can you sit on a couch and have faith that money will come to you and miraculously there it will be?

Yes and no. Money can be a curse and it can be a blessing. Or, money can be a vessel taking you where you want to go or need to be. Money can bring happiness to some and it can be a curse for others.

Money is what you want it to be. And money, like anything else, doesn't just happen. You have to plan, set goals, take action, and have faith, just like anything else you get or achieve in this life.

And, no, you can't sit on a couch and wait for money to fly through the door, it won't happen. Every dream, every goal, every ounce of faith, takes some sort of action.

Money is an important part of our lives. Having it is nice, especially if you have enough to have everything you want and need, and still have a little extra left over to help someone else.

If you are having financial hardships then it is time to take control of your money. It is time to become the master of what you have and set a goal to get more.

What do you have to do to get more money? First, decide what you want. Do you want just enough to pay the bills with a little extra left over? Are you planning to retire and are in the process of pulling your finances together? Do you want to buy a house? Do you want to travel around the world? Do you want to set up trust funds for your children? Do you want to start a business? Think about what you want to do and how much you will need to achieve it.

Once you have a general idea of what you want to do, you have to calculate how much you going to need? Will you need a large sum of money at one time or just a lager monthly income?

Evaluate your situation. How are your financial circumstances right now? Are you comfortable and just need a little (or a lot) more? Or are you scrimping to just put food on the table?

These are the types of questions you should be asking yourself as you set a goal to move forward financially. Money is not just going to come, although it does come in mysterious ways sometimes (keep your eyes open). Plan, set goals, act, and have faith. Faith and action go hand-in-hand.

Having faith is important because you have to believe in your dreams and goals. Faith will give you the motivation you need to move forward. Motivation will guide you to get on that phone, sign up for that class, go to that seminar, write that agent, or get out and meet the right people. Action is the key. Every thing you do is a step toward your dreams, goals, and a brighter financial future.

Money is what you want it to be. Make it a positive force in your life. Get out there and get it, it is waiting for you. Help and motivate others, this will guarantee your own flow of wealth.

And last, don't be afraid to take risks. An abundance of successful people have taken risks and succeeded. Maybe you will not get what you set out to get, but *you tried*. That is worth so much because it means that you will try again and again, until you get what you want. Take the risk. Give yourself a chance at the gold.

If you have evaluated the options, planned, set a goal, and feel ready to take the plunge, then have faith and dive in.

It is up to you to say. **"This is not enough!** I work hard and I expect more from life. I want to enjoy life."** How are you going to achieve this? You are going to start with an abundance of faith. You are going to make plans and set goals. Some of your goals may change over time to reflect new needs that may arise. You are going to stand up, walk out that door, and take action.

- *What do you want*
- *How much do you need to achieve this*
- *Evaluate your financial situation*
- *Be aware of risks and be willing to take them*
- *Motivate yourself to take steps*
- *Believe in what you are doing*
- *Have faith*
- *Help others as you move upward financially*

Chapter 24

Money, Faith, And Me

◆

Let's start with a theory. I'll toss it out for you to explore and decide if it is something you want to believe. *Your memories are all you will take with you on your final journey.* Not one penny will go with you. Nothing you have worked your entire life for will go with you; not your house, car, jewelry or fine clothes. Your bills will be gone and all memories of them wiped from the computers and minds of bill collectors. Bills will be paid or unpaid, and it won't matter either way (not to you anyway). All you will take with you on that final unknown journey is your memories. So, making memories becomes as important as paying bills and making money.

Of course, making memories can sometimes take money. So you have to put things in order of priority and decide when you should be making memories and when you should be making money.

The man who works two jobs and twelve hour shifts has no time for memories. Well not fun, happy memories anyway. Don't let death catch you unprepared with money in the bank, houses, cars, stocks and bonds, but no memories. No warm days at the beach, no hikes to the top of a mountain, no splashing in a lake and no bike rides in the rain. You have to look further then just this life. Work and climb the ladder of success; but stop to enjoy the fruits of your labors as you journey upward.

Memories are the substance of life. When your children are grown they will look back on memories, and so will you. When you go to family gatherings, social events or just out with friends, I'll bet your conversations always come around to some past memory. Things you did as a child, things you and the kids did last week while camping. You will share funny incidents and even sad events. These memories shape us and give us a guide through life.

Have you gone to the beach with your kids and remembered the fun you used to have at the beach when you were a child? When you go shopping does it bring back memories of shopping with your own mother? Can you taste and smell a food you used to love to eat, cotton candy, snow cones, corn on the cob? These are irreplaceable memories. Make memories with your children and someday they will make memories with their own children. Make and share memories with family and friends and give your life real meaning.

You may someday share memories with your grandchildren and great-grandchildren. Rich is the person who has grandparents who has bestowed upon them memories of their past.

Memories are made by the things you do, places you go, things you see, days that are shared with those you love and care about. These activities can be as simple as a day at home making fudge with your three-year-old or reading stories with your ten year old. Memories are a day at the mall with your preteen, a day at the beach or a camping trip. Memories will include the animals we share our lives with; and for some people their animals are their children. Memories are made from the simplest things you could possibly remember. How about waking in the morning smashed between your parents like a bologna sandwich?

Many of us have little money to spare, even for precious memories, so you have to carefully plan activities that require money and skillfully think up activities that are free. An educational walk discovering bugs, roller-skating, mud play, home made clay dough, line dancing, family reunions. Be creative.

Again, as with everything in your life, you need faith. Faith and bills go hand-in-hand. With the power of your faith you will learn and experiment with ways to budget in those trips and activities while still managing the bills. You will realize that somehow, and it isn't our job to question how, but somehow, that electric bill will get paid. Think of it like a baby learning to walk, eventually he will walk, just like eventually all of your bills will get paid. When was the last time you talked to an eighty year old person who still hasn't paid the electric bill from years past?

You should now be in the process of pulling your life together and attempting to get those bills under control. You are slowly moving forward and getting your life where you want it to be. You are learning where your money is going, because you are organizing your financial life, determining your priorities, and setting your goals firmly in front of you.

Bills are a sad part of life. Bills are something we are going to always have. Worrying about bills is unproductive and a waste of energy. Make a plan to get your bills paid. Pay off what you can. Save a little. Then get on with your life and the important things, like making memories. Paying bills is nothing more than a game of strategy. Paying bills can be an exciting venture, as you come up with different and creative strategies toward winning.

Worry does not pay bills. Faith is far more productive and those pesky bills will get paid. Enjoy life, and budget in those special times that will be with you till the end and beyond.

Fact is, no matter what financial worry you have today, will be gone tomorrow. I know you've gotten past last year's money problems, which have probably changed this year. Worry will not contribute one penny toward your bills or your food, so get rid of it! Faith on the other hand has the power to make things happen, even when we can't figure out how it happened.

I am not advocating all play and no work. Those who don't work will never get ahead. Sleeping and watching television all day does not put you on the road to success. Bills do need to be paid. Food does need to be on the table, every day. The children need decent clothes both for school and play. You may have to do overtime or work two jobs to get where you want to be. But, your soul needs to be nourished too. Balance work and play. Work and play both have a place in your life.

Money was never meant for just paying bills, it was meant for making memories and having nice things that make us feel good about our lives and about ourselves.

We all know people who work, and work, and work. They work overtime, they work two jobs, and they work on their days off and on holidays. Invite them on a cruise and they won't be able to go. What a waste of life, memories and money.

The beginning of financial freedom is to DO IT! Make your plans and begin taking steps. Pay the bills and pay yourself. Many of us can use a little more, some of us a lot more. Everyone has money issues, just on different levels. Open your ears and eyes; then listen to what others are doing to gain financial security and freedom. Pick up a few tidbits from everyone; then put the ones you like, and can use, to work in your life. Attend seminars, classes and groups, or read books. Take what you can benefit from and use your new found information to motivate you toward success.

Your most important strategy for getting ahead is to have faith. Listen, learn, put ideas to use and throw worry out the window. Remember, if you are worried, then you are not using your faith. Sit back, take a deep breath, and think about your goals, plans and strategy's for getting where you want to be financially. Eliminate stress and think faith.

Remember the three plans of action, this to will pass, deal with it and do it. This too will pass gives you the freedom to put stress away. No matter how bad your financial situation may seem, it will change. The hard times will end. Nothing remains static.

Deal with it. Pay those bills, pay yourself and make wonderful memories. Deal with each situation and challenge that arises.

Do it means just what it says, **do it.** Play the game of life to its fullest, go with the flow, have faith and combine all of that with hard work.

All the wonderful tools you possess in life, your ability to set goals, the choices you make and your faith, all work together as a team to keep your life in balance, alone they lose their power.

Faith does not pay the bills, you do. Faith gives you the strength to get the job done. Even with faith and hard work you can expect some struggles and challenges. These are just a part of the game of life. Faith gives you the power to face and challenge your struggles.

Having money is great when you learn to control it. Money is a basic need that can bring both pleasure and pain. Where you are financially is no excuse to neglect your dreams, ignore your goals or saturate your life with worry. Weather rich, poor or anywhere in between, everyone can manage to squeeze some memories into their lives. *Do it, have faith and have fun*

Chapter 25

Respect And Appreciation

✦

We all want respect and appreciation. We all want to feel that others appreciate how much we do for them. It is human to want a pat on the back every once in awhile. Most of us rarely get any recognition for the sacrifices we make on a daily basis, and sadly, most of us don't feel like we deserve it anyway.

Does anyone really care that you work double shifts to feed your family, wear cheap ten dollar shoes while the kids wear hundred dollar Nike's? Who notices the hot meal on the table every night? Does anyone ever wonder where the unlimited supple of toilet paper comes from? Probably not!

Why do you think all of these services go unnoticed? Because these are small things others expect and when people expect things they rarely appreciate them. Before others will appreciate you, you have to appreciate yourself. And, when you learn to appreciate yourself, you will begin to respect yourself. When you feel appreciated and respected all of the things you do on a daily basis won't be things you feel you are expected to do, but rather things you want to do.

You are not a martyr when you demand some appreciation. Pat yourself on the back for all you do. It takes a lot to work all day and still manage to get all your other responsibilities completed. Appreciate yourself and others will appreciate you. You do things every day to make the lives of others better, you deserve to be appreciated.

You have dreams and goals beyond housework and cooking. Set priorities for yourself. Allow yourself to be important. Put your goals and dreams higher on your list of things to do.

You do have an obligation to those who are unable to care for themselves such as infants and small children, children and adults with disabilities who are unable to care for themselves, and animals who depend on you, but for everyone else your services are a privilege, not to be mistaken as a right.

When people do show their appreciation, such as a hug from a child or flowers form your spouse, do you blush and act as though you don't deserve the recognition? I hope not because you do. You really do. Take their acts of appreciation as true tokens of all you do for them. You deserve every thank you, every gift, every flower and every hug.

There are those who are givers and those who are takers. Givers don't know how to ask for what they need, their lives evolve around doing for others and not expecting anything in return. Takers take, and take, and never have anything to give back. Both extremes are unhealthy. Your life has to be balanced so you are able to take when you need to and give back when it is needed.

The chronic giver will eventually burn out. And the chronic taker has the potential to abuse and use others for their own gain. Rarely is a chronic giver or a chronic taker, truly happy. A horrible situation would be for a chronic giver to form a relationship with a chronic taker. Beware of these situations!

Beware of either extreme, balance your life. Take charge of what you are willing to give and what you expect back. Give and receive in balance. Give with a happy heart, without expecting anything in return, except a small token of appreciation. And receive graciously, because you deserve it.

Your life is entwined with all the people you care about (and even those you pass through life) and should be a mixture of mutual give and take. If no one is willing to give to you, then you will have to give to yourself in order to keep the balance. Life is a series of give and take between people; it is about appreciating and respecting each other.

Chapter 26

Demands And Sacrifices

✦

The numbers of women who work outside the home have grown significantly in recent years. The ideal was once centered on the stay-at-home mom, who cared for the children while dad worked outside the home to support the family. With the increase of non-traditional homes, such as single parent, adoptions, divorce, grandparents raising grandchildren, this ideal has changed.

More women are in the work force and more men are becoming stay at home dads, and this is acceptable in our culture today. Men and women are working equally outside the home and as homemakers; two tough roles to combine.

Women are getting higher degrees than in the past. Men are taking on roles that were unheard of at one time. And all of this is combined into a very productive, but busy and fast paced life style for most people.

Running a home with its never-ending demands and sacrifices is a life consuming job. It wears into you mentally, physically, and spiritually. Most people, after a long day at work, go home not to a hot bath, but to a pile of laundry, a sink full of dishes, a hungry family, soccer practice, a messy house, or classes at the local college. All of these demands must be met, which for most of us means cutting into our after work hours and days off.

Life's fast pace may leave you feeling isolated from others. You may go from work to home and back to work again (sleep is optional.) The key is to balance *you*. It doesn't matter if you work outside the home or not, you must find a balance in order to pace your life.

Because you do live life on the fast track and because everyday is a whirlwind of constant obligations and responsibilities, you may find yourself, at times, hating your life and even those closest to you. If you feel this way, something is wrong. Even in this fast paced life and even with all of your responsibilities, you should still find some measure of satisfaction and happiness. This issue must be addressed, possibly through therapy, possibly through your own personal resources. Never allow unhappiness to become a part of your life. Something is wrong and it is something that must be addressed before you can fill your gas tank (your mental reserves) and move on.

If you become overwhelmed, tired or depressed, this could be situational and within a reasonable period of time you should return to a normal state of functioning. If you become depressed and are unable to move back to a normal state, then there is a problem. Learning the signs of burnout is essential.

Burnout is a constant feeling of unhappiness. Burnout blocks your ability to get any satisfaction out of life. Those you love become a burden and your life is a burden. You may become verbally and /or physically abusive to your children, yourself, or others. You are suffering from burn-out.

We spoke earlier of paying yourself. You need time for yourself, as well as time for your family and friends. Your life cannot revolve around work, school, and kids. You owe yourself and you have to pay yourself or nature will step in, and the result will be burnout and depression.

Take care of yourself for your peace of mind. Take care of yourself for those you care about. Take care of yourself so you are as productive as you can be both at home and on the job.

What ever you give to yourself or do for yourself, **you deserve!** You spend hours, days, weeks and months out of every year taking care of others. What about you? If you burnout and become immobilized due to depression or some other debilitating emotional disorder, you will not able to give one hundred percent of yourself to all the things that are important to you.

Your life is a series of roles, you are: chuffer, cook, Gardner, counselor, judge, maid, coach, therapist, employee, mother, daughter, son, and father, the roles are endless. Take a moment to sit down and write what you do everyday, both emotionally and physically, for those close to you, and even those not close to you. Learn to appreciate yourself and pay yourself. You deserve it spiritually, emotionally, and physically. How often do you pay yourself? As often as you feel you need and as often as you want. Once a week, once a month, there is no limit to what you owe yourself.

Life is a challenge and it becomes twice the challenge when you have children. Life is also rewarding, especially when you have children. All of the rewards and challenges become a part of your story. You are the hero or heroine of your story. No amount of money, gold, silver or diamonds can ever add up to your true value. You are priceless.

Anyone striving to get ahead in life is going to, at some point, become overwhelmed with the demands on their life and on their time. The sacrifices you make on a daily basis will quickly build into huge mountains. Burnout will hover over your head. This is all a part of your journey.

Any time you feel defeated, sad, depressed or overwhelmed, pull off the road and evaluate your life. You may need to rethink your goals. You may have to take smaller steps and that's okay because you are still moving forward. Balance your life. Your journey is not always going to be easy, but it will always be exciting, as you make turns at blind corners or wind around thrilling and unknown territory.

Look at your journey not as a series of struggles and hardships, but as a thrilling adventure with exciting challenges. Be excited about each new adventure, even the ones that are unexpected. You are living life to the fullest and that can never be bad.

Chapter 27

Success

✦

What does success mean to you? Is it having a great job, a luxury car, a huge house, money in the bank, a nice retirement, stocks, bonds, extra cash in your pocket, being surrounded by family and friends, or traveling? In short, success is what ever you perceive it to be.

Think of a homeless person who has a nice basket, a special corner to sleep on, and a place to shower once in a while; is he happy? If the answer for him is yes, then he has found a measure of success for himself.

What about the man who has a small house and a meager savings? He is surrounded by family and friends. His family loves to camp and play soccer. His wife stays at home and cares for the kids while he goes to work at a fast food joint; is he happy? You bet he is; he has what he wants in life; he has achieved success.

The man who lives in a mansion and has a large bank account is happy, the guy doing a long haul in prison may be happy. How do you define success? Success is something you have to define for yourself. For me, success is when you are satisfied with what you have achieved in life and feel truly happy and blessed; then you have discovered the meaning of success.

Goals are a priority, because goals motivate you into action. No one does something for nothing, there is always a payoff. Success is a positive payoff for working toward your goals and for sacrificing immediate pleasures for future rewards. Success has two components; there has to be a goal and there has to be motivation. Together, goals and motivation are powerful forces. On your journey there are going to be obstacles, sacrifices, and challenges. When you plan your goals think about what success is to you and how much you are willing to risk and sacrifice to have it. Happiness and success is the final outcome of your dreams, goals, and hard work.

As time moves on, and as you grow and change with each new experience, your goals and your definition of success will change, and that is okay. Do not allow your life to become static. Change can be (and is) a positive force.

The homeless person who is perfectly content on the corner today, may tomorrow decide he wants to have a real home. The rich person may decide to give up all of his material possessions and travel to Africa to live and work in a rural village. Changing your ideas of what success means to you, and changing your goals is okay, that is what keeps your life fluid and exciting. Success is moving toward what ever it is you want to do or be at any given moment in your life. Success is happiness and happiness is success.

While striving toward your goals and dreams, stop occasionally to remind yourself of how special, unique, and blessed you are. Take a few moments, even just once a month, to appreciate what you have, no matter how small it may seem. We all have special gifts that have been bestowed upon us at birth, either for our own pleasures or to share with others. Many of us haven't discovered what that unique talent or gift is. Stop and take the time to think about all you have already achieved in this life because of your special talent or gift. Writing, art, leadership qualities, sports, mathematical genius, and speaking abilities are all examples of special gifts. Without realizing it these gifts might be responsible for the work you are doing, the desire you have to help others or the hobbies you pursue. These are blessings. Become aware of your special gifts or talents and use them to your advantage.

Success is measured by your own interpretation of what success is. Every one of us begins life with the capability and the necessary tools to achieve success. From birth we are given the roots of our future gifts, our special talents. It is up to the adults in the child's life to nurture these talents and gifts until the child is old enough to make the choice of how he or she will use their own unique gifts.

We are heirs, from birth, to all of the wonders of nature. Not one child born is left out. This inheritance is the beginning of success. Nature doesn't understand homelessness, poor, rich, mental illness or handicapped. Nature is blind to the house you live in, the car you drive, or the size of your bank account. In nature we are all equal, money is obsolete. Nature is free, there for you to use as you wish, to expand your world and the world of those you love and care about. Give your children a love of nature and it will last through out their life time, and the lifetime of their own children and grandchildren.

Bestow upon the children in your life, your sons, daughters, grandchildren, nieces and nephews a love of learning; the most valuable gift you can give to them. Stimulate their sense of curiosity. Give your children the world as their classroom and watch them blossom. Push children from the very beginning of their lives toward success.

Your potential for success is unlimited. You have so much to work with. You have the gift of sight, hearing, strong legs, and healthy bodies. You have material possessions, your house, car, and boat. You are blessed with your children, family, friends, and special talents. These are all gifts. When you begin to appreciate how much you already possess; you will realize how successful you already are, and have always been. The tools that you may not have realized existed will now become obvious to you.

It is about appreciating the world you live in. It is about appreciating how your children, family and friends have enriched your life; even in the worst of times. It is realizing how blessed you are to have so much. This is what life is all about; having so much and learning to appreciate and savor all of it. And, you are even more blessed to have the choices of how you will spend your time enjoying and using all of your gifts. This is success.

Life is exhilarating and having others to enjoy it with is a treasure unsurpassed by all others. Take a walk, jog, or hike. Go outside and watch the sun set. One gift to yourself is well worth your time. One gift to yourself is a gift to all those who surround you. When you are filled with joy; those close to you share in the joy that you are experiencing.

When you feel at peace; those around you feel that peace and it becomes a part of them. When you're happy; others are happy. When you're stress free; others are stress free.

Life's abundance of gifts can be enjoyed alone or shared with others. You have a lifetime to discover and enjoy the gifts the world offers to you. There is no rush, but don't wait too long to make these majestic gifts a part of your journey. When you open yourself to all the riches you possess, then, and only then, can you begin to really appreciate what life is handing to you.

Time is a precious commodity; you have an abundance of it, but will never use all of it; so use what you have wisely. What is here today will be here tomorrow; there is no perfect time. Time is precious, valuable, and always here. How you chose to use your time is your choice. How you want to use your gifts that life has given to you is your choice. If you chose to use your time sleeping, drugged out, locked away from the world, drowning in depression, hating and hurting others, or whining about how unfair life is, that is your choice. You have gifts, choices and time; put the three together and use them to open your world or use them too find reasons to complain about life. Some people go through life and never use their gifts at all. They allow random events to make all of their choices for them. Their time is wasted on empty days, loneliness and unbearable hours. This is their choice, and sadly, their measure of success.

Learn to appreciate life and all of its gifts. Use your time in ways that will enhance your life. Make choices that will give you the most return on your time and gifts. And, give your children the knowledge that they too have been given an abundance of gifts at birth, that will last a lifetime, and one of those gifts is the gift of time. Your children have time to pursue their goals and dreams, and to live a life of abundant happiness. Time goes on into eternity; use every minute given to you until your last day here on earth. The most challenging of all your gifts is the gift of choice.

When traveling the road of life stop once in a while to really explore where you have been and to look at what lies ahead. Take everything life offers you, especially the free stuff and enjoy your journey to your ultimate destination, success and happiness.

Chapter 28

Make It Happen

✦

Nothing is going to happen unless you make it happen. Life will continue every day, just like the day before, until you see a problem and want to change it.

If you argue with your husband, every single day, then in ten years you are still going to be arguing with your husband, probably about the same issues; unless you change it. Are your kids disrespecting you? They will continue to disrespect you, until you change it. Do you need more money? Financially, no matter how much time passes, you will still be in a financial slump, unless you change it. You have to want to make a change. Write down all of your possibilities and options, talk to others, read books, plan on how that change will happen, set positive goals and then act.

Doing the same things day in and day out that is not working will never work. You have to be willing to make changes. You have to be willing to take risks. You have to be willing to come out of your comfort zone.

Changes in your life will be both huge and small. All changes require the same steps: Faith, choices, plans and action. Take tiny steps, until you feel comfortable with the changes in your life. There is no rush and no possibility of failure, because you are making positive choices that can be manipulated and changed at any time.

Yes, you are in a comfort zone. As much as the kids' screaming while you are trying to study annoys you, you are still used to it and somehow manage to get your studying done. But how about something simple, a small step that might change that everyday scene? An example: Sit the kids down and have a short but effective talk with them. "Every Wednesday, from three to five in the afternoon, I will be studying. I expect it to be quite during those hours." When Wednesday rolls around and it is apparent that the kids are not going to respect your wish, you simply pack your school supplies up, get into the car, drive to the library and study there for two hours.

This routine will continue until the kids finally realize that you are serious or until you realize that the library is a much nicer place to study. At any rate, you have changed the self defeating scenario (that was never going to change) that prevented you from studying; you have now opened the door to positive change. This is only one example as to how simple the changes can be. There are hundreds of other ideas, limited to nothing more than your own imagination.

If you continue to do the same things, then things will stay the same. Don't expect change if you aren't willing to change it. Remember, **nothing is going to happen unless you make it happen.** This can be applied to anything and everything in your life.

Changes are possible, but you have to make them happen.

Anything causing you stress or unhappiness is a potential situation for change. No change is possible unless you act. Your life is in your hands. You have the power to make changes. Decide to make the changes you want to see in your life, then do it.

Chapter 29

Getting Things Done

✦

Living life is exciting, thrilling, and challenging, but it can also be a lot of hard work. Living today in this fast paced age of computers, electronics, and other high powered gadgets can make your daily life even more complicated and confusing. It doesn't matter if you work outside the home or are a stay-at-home mom or dad. You are on call twenty-four hours a day, seven days a week. Sadly, no matter what you do or how much time you spend doing it, nothing seems to get done. The hours you spend working, sacrificing, and doing for others may seem like wasted time.

Being in constant motion, yet, getting nothing done is a part of living. This should be a motivator for you to learn how to organize your time and your resources.

Everyday holds something magical for you to see and something special for you to learn. Don't look at your days as boring, tedious, unending, or draining. Look for the magic in every single day. Life is how you look at it. Every single day is brand new, even if it seems to be the same as the day before. Treat each new day as novel and not as an extension of the previous day.

The reality is beds need to be made every day. Laundry needs to be washed every day. Kids get dirty and need baths every day. Then it starts again. There will be cups in the sink immediately after you put the last one into the dishwasher. The bills continue to pile up, there are rugs to vacuum, furniture to dust, groceries to buy, and soccer practice. Not to mention all of your daily responsibilities at work.

Since you are aware that some aspects of your life are going to be tedious and unending, there is only one solution and that is to do what you can or absolutely have to do for your own peace of mind. If you cannot leave your house unless every bed is made; then make all the beds and ignore the things that don't bother you. If you can't stand for dirty dishes to pile up; then wash the dishes and move on. If a dirty carpet drives you crazy; then vacuum. Do what you have to do to feel satisfied; then move on. Don't get hung up in what doesn't have to be done this very minute. If you want to do dishes only on Saturdays; then do dishes only on Saturdays.

You are the judge on what or how much you can leave for another time, and how much you have to accomplish right now in order to capture that feeling of satisfaction. When you feel satisfied; then you will be ready to move on to other tasks. Pace yourself.

Don't confuse doing what only makes you feel satisfied with procrastination. Everything has to get done, but on your terms. Remember, your goal is to be stress free so you can move though life, accomplish your goals, and live your dreams. Tedious, daily chores are a very small part of your life; don't turn them into mountains.

Priorities are putting things in an order that gives you a feeling of accomplishment and satisfaction, thus leaving you feeling stress free and excited about moving on. Every day there will be things that have to be done, it can be as simple as doing a sink full of dishes to a major business deal. Your job is to prioritize what has to be done, and what you realistically want or need to do, in the time frame you have available to you. Eventually, everything of any importance will get done. Strive for balance.

We all have a comfort zone when it comes to daily chores. Organize those boring chores and tackle them when you know deep down inside that it is time. And you'll know when the time has come, it's a gut feeling. It's not about Aunt Sue believing beds should be made everyday, it's about you and weather or not the unmade beds bother you. I can't stand dishes to pile up in my sink so I wash them everyday. I have a friend who doesn't care how high the dishes pile up, so her sink stays full.

The good news is that once you reach your comfort zone (when it comes to getting chores done) you can really enjoy whatever activity you choose to do with your kids, friends, or spouse, and they will sense that you really want to be there. For those of us who have smaller comfort zones, it is going to mean less time for the ones you care about, but, I guarantee you, they will survive.

Have faith. You are doing fine. Now move on.

Chapter 30

Where Am I Going

✦

We all face mountains in life. We have questions. Where am I? Where do I want to go? How will I get there? Who do I want to be? Who hasn't at least once in life, felt like life has kicked them in the rear and left them in the cold with no where to turn? We have all been victims to the annoying voices in our heads that tell us we are not smart enough, pretty enough, rich enough or thin enough.

That little, irritating voice in your head may have you believing that you will never go back to school for that masters degree; there are just too many obstacles. You will never own the home of your dreams; you will never have the money for the down payment and even if you do somehow come up with the down payment, how are you going to make the house note? You will never get over a major loss; so keep swimming in that pool of despair and loneliness, your life is over. Your goals are a waste of time; you don't need goals to get things done. Dreams are for children; they rarely come true, except for the very rich.

The time has come to stand up to those pesky voices from your past. It is time to listen to a new voice, the voice of faith. The voice that tells you how valuable you are, that cheers you on and is excited about your goals and dreams. The voice of faith assures you that dreaming, planning and acting will put you on the right path; the path that will take you from where you are right now to where you want to be. **If you**

are facing in the right direction all you have to do is walk. Walk to your life of happiness, success and fulfilled desires.

Faith and action are the foundation of your journey. On your journey you will be bombarded with an abundance of blessings. **YEAH!** You are ready to face challenges in order to achieve all you are entitled to in life. The challenges are the exciting part of your journey. Challenges motivate you and make you stronger as time passes. Challenges are life lessons.

Your dreams, goals, challenges and journey will be full of choices. There are no wrong choices. Life is a moving entity and everything can be changed, because your thoughts can be changed.

Where are you going? You are going where you want to go. You are going where your dreams and goals take you. Sometimes, you may come to a place you didn't want to be, take your time and make sure it is not a better place then what you had planned. Life gives us choices, but sometimes she takes us on another path we never would have thought about. If it is not where you want to be then plan, set new goals and move on. When you are ready, sit down and say," I am truly blessed," then you will be on the right path.

Take risks, try unknown adventures, experiment with new options and dream big. Life does not end after we get all we think we want or need; there is always more. Your goals and dreams should be never-ending until your very last day on this earth.

Everyday is a beginning. Don't wait for an end. You are never too old to dream and never too young to have goals.

Part Five

Live, Learn, Grow

✦

Chapter 31

Wisdom

✦

Words are powerful. I have included in this section some wonderful words of wisdom from sources that include Yiddish proverbs and inspirational words. These are short and simple words that I hope you will carry with you on your journey through life. These words and thoughts are filled with wisdom, inspiration, and hope. Keep these words close to your heart for quick pick-me-ups' and strength.

These wonderful passages are not my own, but passages that I have found through other sources to be especially powerful. These words have the ability to give you the power you need to live life to the fullest, survive hard times or to just savor the beauty of life.

I cannot give you every source that was used because some of these gems came from unknown sources, but I do want to thank every person who contributed to this chapter to help us grow as human beings.

Use this chapter when you need an extra push. Use this chapter when you feel weak and vulnerable. Use this chapter to give you the strength you may need to move on during hard times. Use this chapter when you need a daily lift. Use this chapter just for the joy of it.

And, write down some of your own thoughts, verses or words of others that were especially powerful for you. You can never have too much strength while on your journey.

INSPIRATION

When you come to the edge of all the light you know and are about to step off into the darkness of the unknown, faith is knowing one of two things will happen: there will be something solid to stand on, or you will be taught how to fly.
Barbara J. Winter

Life is like a trumpet. If you don't put anything in, you won't get anything out.
W.C. Handy

I bend, but I do not break.
Jean De La Fontaine

There are no mistakes, no coincidences. All events are blessings given to us to learn from.
Elizabeth Kubler-Ross

For just one day, forget about tomorrow so that you may fully experience today.
Corita Ken

The mind should be like a camera-loaded with appreciation, ready to capture in full color and perfect focus the essence of each beautiful moment.
Jim Beggs

It is never too late to be what you might have become.
George Eliot

There is nothing stronger in the world then gentleness.
Han Suyin

I've shut the door on yesterday, and thrown the key away- tomorrow holds no fears for me, since I have found today.
Vivian Yeiser Laramore

Take rest; a field that has rested gives a bountiful crop.
Ovid

Seek always the answer from within.
Eileen Caddy

There is no medicine like hope, no incentive so great and no tonic as powerful as the expectation of something tomorrow.
O.S. Marden

Faith is the substance of things hoped for, the evidence of things not seen.
Hebrews 11:1

Where there is great love there are always miracles.
Willa Cather

Dreams come true; without that possibility, nature would not incite us to have them.
John Updike

On earth there is no heaven, but there are pieces of it.
Jules Renard

Seek not outside yourself; heaven is within.
Mary Lou Cook

All things are possible to him that believes.
Mark 9:23

Heaven gives its glimpses only to those not in the position to look to close.
Robert Frost

Heaven is the place where the donkey at last catches up with the carrot.
Anonymous

It has never been my object to record my dreams, just the determination to realize them.
Man Ray

One miracle is just as easy to believe as another.
William Jennings Bryan

First we have to believe, and then we believe.
G.C. Lichtenberg

It takes only one person to change your life-You.
Ruth Casey

You will find your strength within you; in places deep inside that you have not yet dared to visit.
Ruth Fishel

Be still and listen to the stillness within.
Darlene Larson Jenks

No day in which you learn something is a complete loss.
David Eddings

Childhood is measured by sounds, smells, and sights, before the dark hour of reason grows.
John Betjeman

Nothing is as frustrating as arguing with someone who knows what he's talking about.
Sam Ewing

There's no way to be a perfect mother and a million ways to be a good one.
Jill Churchill

Action is the antidote to despair.
Joan Baez

Be not forgetful to entertain strangers for thereby some have entertained angels unawares.
Hebrews 13:2

It's not how much we have, but how much we enjoy that makes happiness.
Charles Haddon Spurgeon

When we do the best we can, we never know what miracles are wrought in our life, or in the life of another.
Helen Keller

Loving ourselves creates miracles in our lives
Louise Hay

Don't be afraid to take big steps. You can't cross a chasm in two small leaps.
David George Lloyd

There are always two voices sounding in our ears-the voice of fear and the voice of confidence. One is the clamor of the senses; the other is the whispering of the higher self.
Charles B. Newcomb

Know that you have all that you need to do all that is good and right in your life today.
Ruth Fishel

What a strange pattern the shuttle of life can weave.
Frances Marion

Faith is the daring of the soul to go farther then it can see.
William Newton Clark

Do you count your birthdays thankfully?
Horace

Love builds highways out of dead ends.
Louis Gittner

To have grown wise and kind is real success.
Anonymous

And in today already walks tomorrow.
Samuel Taylor Coleridge

Enthusiasm is the yeast that makes your hopes rise to the stars.
Henry Ford

A multitude of small delights constitutes happiness.
Charles Baudelaire

Among those whom I like or admire, I can find no common denominator, but among those whom I love, I can: All of them make me laugh.
W.H. Auden

A father is a man who expects his children to be as good as he meant to be.
Carolyn Coats

The life you have led doesn't need to be the only life you have.
Anne Quindien

Truth is eternal, knowledge is changeable. It is disastrous to confuse them.
Madeleine L'Engle

The trail is the thing, not the end of the trail. Travel too fast and you miss all you are traveling for.
Louis L'Amour

Flowers are the sweetest things God ever made and forgot to put a soul into.
Henry Ward Beecher

The man who views the world at 50 the same as he did at 20 has wasted 30 years of his life.
Muhammad Ali

People see God every day, they just don't recognize him.
Pearl Bailey

Shared joy is double joy, and shared sorrow is half sorrow.
Swedish Proverb

To love is to receive a glimpse of Heaven.
Karen Sunde

God gives, but man must open his hand.
German proverb

If you are facing in the right direction, all you have to do is walk.

Everything in life has meaning, the bigger the fall the greater the lesson.

Expect miracles.

Don't quit before the miracle.

You fall down seven times, you get up eight.

YIDDISH PROVERBS

A wicked tongue is worse than an evil hand.

Mountains cannot meet, but men can.

A little charm and you are not ordinary.

It's a good idea to send a lazy man for the Angel of Death.

A friend you get for nothing; an enemy has to be bought.

A baby is born with clenched fists and a man dies with his hands open.

A man should stay alive if only out of curiosity.

Lost years are worst than lost dollars.

The tongue is the pen of the heart.

The reddest apple has a worm in it.

When things go right you become rich.

Trying to please is always costly.

It doesn't cost anything to promise and to love.

Every man has his burden.

Chapter 32

Blessings

✦

Your life is overflowing with blessings, no matter who you are or what your life circumstances may be. When you begin to realize how much you have and how blessed you have been, you will begin to apprehend your full potential in life. You will know, without a doubt, that someone or something, a force greater than yourself, who ever or what ever that force may be for you, is out there and taking care of you. Life happens; let it happen and then decorate it to make it exactly what you want it to be. Nothing is off limits and nothing is lost when you are living life.

Blessings are all of the material possessions that are a part of your life. Blessings can also be feelings, wisdom, a special talent, the opportunity to engage in work where you are productive, or having a special person or animal in your life. There is no limit to the magnitude of your blessings.

If you sit down and list all of your blessings, the list would be endless; from the moon in the sky, to the house you live in, the endless mountains, millions of trees, rivers, our children, grandchildren, nieces, nephews, our hands, feet, eyes. The list goes on and on. Do you think you could ever come to the end of a blessing list?

No one is without an abundance of blessings. There are countless people who have no idea of the blessings that overflow in their lives.

Some will come to the end of their journey and never have truly enjoyed or realized their blessings.

If you aren't aware of all of your blessings, then you aren't aware of all of the potential you have in your life. If you have suffered a loss, are going through hardships, are searching for meaning in your life, want to set goals and dreams that you can believe in and achieve, then you have to start with faith and with the knowledge that your life is filled with blessings. Your life is powerful because you have so many blessings available to guide you and to help you succeed in anything you choose to do or become.

Stop and count your blessings. Stop and think about the blessings that you haven't even tapped into yet. When you run out of gas or have a flat tire, and a stranger lends a helping hand; it's a blessing. When you get a job you absolutely love; it's a blessing. When your kids make you proud; it's a blessing. When you have the ability to set goals and achieve them; it's a blessing. Sitting at home in front of a fireplace, with the dog at your feet, and the kid's tucked snugly in bed is a blessing.

Blessings give you power. Blessings are abundant, knowing neither rich nor poor, black or white, pretty or homely. Not one person alive is without blessings in their lives.

Without even asking for them, you are given an abundance of blessings at birth. Can you imagine what would happen if you began to seek out all of your blessings? When you set goals and dream dreams, you are opening yourself to blessings.

Faith and blessings work hand-in-hand. Together they give you power. You are unstoppable. You can overcome any issues, hardships, pain, or sorrow that may arise in your life. You have the power to set any goal or dream any dream. There are no limits to where your life can go.

Count the blessings that are already a part of your life. Set goals and make other blessings happen. Have faith and believe that your life will come together, and not be a burden that you must endure for eighty or ninety years.

Blessings happen. Life happens. Become an active participant in the writing of your life story by having faith, setting goals, dreaming dreams, and watching all of your blessings come to life.

Give your blessings life. Take what is given to you and know that you deserve it. Life is not meant to be unhappy, stressful, unproductive, or boring. Life is meant to be fun, exciting, vibrant, and full of everything you could ever want or need. Life is the sun setting and the moon rising; meant to be lived from sun up to sun down. Life is full of love, laughter, prosperity and thrilling adventures, to name a few. But, life is limited. There is little time to enjoy everything that is available to you. You have to live life now, while it is here. Life is short; it will be gone in the wink of an eye.

Take the good and treasure it. Take the bad and learn from it. And, take both the good and the bad to help others, so they too can travel this wondrous journey.

Chapter 33

You Are Important

✦

You are important. You are the foundation of your family, the heart of your home. You make a difference where you work. You give something to those you pass everyday, even with just a smile that says I care.

Your compassion for others and your zest for life are apparent. Examine your values and beliefs and use that knowledge to better your life and the life of another.

Take care of you, for yourself and for those you love and care about. Don't downplay your importance at home or at work.

You are here for a purpose. That purpose is to live the life that was given to you. You were not blessed with this wonderful experience solely to make you unhappy and miserable. It is not coincidence that this fascinating experience, called life, exists. It is a possibility that what happens in this life is the foundation of your next life. Enjoy this magical encounter.

The most important job you have before beginning your journey is to understand and believe how important you are. On your journey you will be given opportunities that you may not have realized existed. Everything is in front of you, open your eyes and believe in *you*. Opportunities to better your life both materially, emotionally and spiritually are knocking at your door, **right now,** open the door. This is reality. You are just now discovering that you were born rich. **How wonderful!**

When your life is balanced, when you have set goals and made plans on how you will achieve those goals, when you dream huge dreams and believe that they are going to happen, then you are beginning to realize how important you are, to yourself and to everyone around you. Life is not an accident. Life happens. Be a part of this life, not sad and depressed, but filled with positive energy, ready to face each new day and each new challenge.

Sadness and tragedy happens and you will survive. You will feel pain, and you will feel powerless. Let it happen, and when you are ready, let it go.

Evaluate your situation, set goals, and act. Move. Make choices. Nothing will happen unless you make it happen. Make things happen. Make choices that will move you forward toward a successful and prosperous life.

Don't look at life as though it is a dull, boring drama that you are forced to be a part of. Life has a meaning much deeper than any of us may ever know. Live life while it is happening. Have faith, have fun, live life.

You are important. You are special. You are capable. You are beautiful. Love You.

Chapter 34

Final Thoughts, But Not The End

✦

Now let's pull it all together. You have hopefully, by now, begun to trust in the power of faith. If you don't feel confident that faith will carry you, when you are too tired to walk, then keep working toward the goal of believing and trusting in your faith. In time, you will feel the difference and know that faith is truly working in your life.

Your strength and power will come from the foundation you will build using faith, patience, and perseverance. With faith you take the problem off of you and put it in the hands of another power; whatever that power may be for you.

Patience gives you the freedom of time. Once you have made a choice or set a goal, let it go and let it happen. Have you tapped into your patience? Has using the power of patience made life a little easier for you? Is life a little less stressful now that you don't have to impatiently wait for things to happen? With patience you can take steps, move forward, set goals and then put it away until the miracle happens.

With perseverance you will learn to hold on to your faith as fate does her job. Never ever give up. Have you been practicing your perseverance? Do you now realize that success takes time, but it will come? If you are setting goals, believing in those goals, dreaming dreams, taking steps forward and having faith, then you are moving in the right direction. Persevere and believe that things are going to happen.

There are three basic acts you will use over and over again. Number one is: *do it.* When you have a decision to make or something that needs to get done, be it washing the dishes or signing up for classes at the college, don't procrastinate, don't wonder if it is right or wrong, don't worry about money or other incidentals, just DO IT! Get things done. Make things happen. Do it and keep doing it (whatever goal you have set for yourself) until you have everything you want, until all of your dreams have been realized, and until all of your goals have been met. Do whatever it is that you have to do to make your life as satisfying and exciting as it can possibly be.

Number two is: *deal with it.* There is nothing in this world that you will face, good or bad, that you won't have to deal with in one way or another. You may choose to deal with your situation in a destructive way or in a positive way, but every act has to be dealt with sooner or later. So, deal with it. Deal with life. Life can be overwhelming, but no matter what tragedy life hands to you, no mater how horrible, you are going to have to deal with life on some level. Make choices that will keep you moving no matter how horrible that life event might be. You can and will stay in control. Use your faith and the power you have inside of you to deal with life in a positive way. Take what ever horror has passed through your life and use it to mode your life into something positive. And, use your own happy moments and even your tragedies to help others who may be suffering or struggling.

Number three, *this too will pass,* is meant to fill you with hope. It will also make you realize how special happy times are with your friends, family, favorite pet, and even alone. All things pass. No matter how life shattering or how glorious; all events in life will pass. Time marches on, children grow old, and every trial, tribulation, challenge, and joy in your life will pass and fade into a memory, leaving another mark on your existence and another chapter in your book. Use the bad times to learn and grow from, and embrace the good times. Make wonderful memories for future generations and as a reminder of how wonderful this life is.

Life hands you many challenges and all of these challenges become a tiny bit of who you are. You have the ability and the freedom to make hundreds of choices as you pass through life. There is no right or wrong way to deal with any of the issues that pop up in you life. Every choice you make will have a consequence, taking you down new and exciting roads. If the road you take isn't what you wanted or expected then turn around and take another route or you can stay where you are at, open your eyes, discover all of the possibilities, and make it a positive experience. But, never stop. Every choice you make will affect your life and sometimes the lives of others. Make choices that will make you happy, successful, and prosperous. What ever choice you make; something will always happen. You have the power to change and mold your life through choices

Every person writes their own story. Each chapter in your life will have a beginning, middle, and an end. Some chapters will be happy and fun, while others will be sad or lonely. All add to the magic of life. Someday each and every one of us will write our last chapter. You will make memories and these are the only things that you will take with you to the grave. So, make an abundance of memories and you will live on forever in the lives of your grandchildren, your great-grandchildren, and beyond.

Be kind and empathetic to those you pass in life. Give what you can to those you can help and leave a little happiness or a ray of hope to those in need. Know that there will be someone there to help you too, when you need it.

A favorite verse of mine from the Bible and a powerful foundation to build your life on is: *That which you give, so you shall receive.* If you plant a good harvest, then you can expect to get good and rich fruits back. If you plant weeds, then you will harvest weeds. Plant a huge, beautiful, colorful, vibrant garden. Be kind to others and help them whenever you can. Helping others is more than an obligation, it is an opportunity. Others depend on vessels to pass through their lives, just as you do. Become a vessel for others, but always be on the look out for your own vessel to come past when you need it. Nothing you do is ever done in vain, it will always come back. Plant roses and harvest roses. Plant weeds and harvest weeds.

Life is not always kind. Don't expect it to be. Be willing to face the challenges and obstacles that life will hand to you; this is what will make your story unique and exciting. Life gives you treasures and gifts beyond your wildest dreams, but expects something back from you, something simple; help your fellow traveler when you see that they are in need.

You have all you will ever need in this life, family, friends, nature, challenges, and adventures. Everything you need is here, for your unlimited use, but you have to take it.

No man is an island. We are here for each other and your actions do affect others.

Worry and stress should exist only in a small corner of your mind, only to act as a warning device, which should rarely have to be activated. Reach for your dreams and have goals. Dream it, believe it, plan it, go for it, and take it.

Remember, you are not perfect, you are human and you will act human. You may yell too much, curse too much, or do other things that are not always nice. You are human. You will make mistakes and that's okay. You may do things others don't approve of and that's okay too, as long as it doesn't interfere with the well being of others.

There are few truly evil, bad people in this life. Most people are writing their own stories and in the process they may hurt others, but they can be forgiven and move on, because life moves on. Life is fluid, giving you the chance to start over again, and again, until you get what you want.

Be happy. What ever makes you happy; do it. What ever you want to do in this life; do it. If you are happy living under a bridge, live there. If you want a mansion, get one. There is nothing stopping you from reaching for and achieving your most desired goals and dreams, *except you*. Everything you need to prosper and move forward in this life is out there. Find it, take it, and use it to your advantage

Hate, anger, and life long grudges, will hold you back and zap you of positive energy; be aware of this. Negative feelings, although a normal part of life, will drain you of the energy you are going to need to navigate through life. You are human and will have negative feelings. Negative feelings do have a place in this life, but don't allow these feelings to dominate your life. Feel and understand your anger, then jump back into life. Get your hands a little dirty, face challenges, take risks, and **Live life**. Don't waste needless energy on hating others or holding grudges that go on for years. Someone owes you money? Okay, be pissed then move on; you will probably never get it back. Someone hurt you? Okay, experience the pain and then move on. Nothing will ever change because of anger and hate. Time and energy are valuable commodities. Feel the pain, the anger, the hate, the frustration, and then move on.

How about that age old demon, money? Well, the truth is, we need money. Life is better with money. Most people want money, even just a little. Most people want to drive a nice car, wear nice clothes, and enjoy all the other amenities of life, and that is okay. Wanting material things motivates us to move forward and act. Money is a powerful motivator for many people. If you get a lot of it (and I know you will) don't forget the poor. Be humble. Remember, those you pass going up, are those you pass coming down. Everyone wants to move up in life, but if you are content to be poor in this life, that's okay. Build the framework of your life where you want to be. If you don't choose to have riches and material wealth, then build your life with what you feel you need and want. *Your* happiness is your number one concern.

Everything you do in life is okay, as long as you are aware of what you want and you don't intentionally hurt anyone on your journey to where you want to be.

If a poor man living on the streets is happy, he has achieved his dream. If you would rather have a large house and a maid, then go for it. What ever you want is there for the taking. Take what you want and give a little back to others.

Life begs no one to embrace her. You have to be willing to embrace life and only then will life embrace you back. The earth needs energy from people who embrace life, who live life, and who have as much to give as they take.

A person dying of a terminal illness can embrace life. A person struggling from day to day can embrace life. It's an attitude. It's the desire to live and enjoy all that life has to offer. It's appreciating all you have and believing in everything that is yet to come.

You will cry and experience tremendous pain in your life. Some people, sadly, will bear more pain and have more burdens to carry than others; there is no answer for this. No one who has faith will be given more than they can handle. You are stronger than you probably know.

Whatever life hands you is your story. Your story will be written weather you choose to control where it goes or not. Your story will touch the lives of others in ways you may never know. No one wants a life full of unhappiness, failure, and tears, but it is a part of the human condition. Everyone, including you, will experience both pain and happiness in life and you will survive. Remember the bad that passes through your life and use it to learn from, and embrace the good times and moments that are also a part of your life.

Accept life as it comes to you. Change it and manipulate it as you choose, because this is what will give your life power. You possess the freedom of choice and the power to use it anytime you desire. **Use it.** Life is meant to be lived; you cannot sleep through life.

One of life's most precious gifts is your children. Value them. Don't try to be perfect parents, try only to be good parents, most children will survive. Your children have their own life stories to write. Children know when they are loved and valued. The foundation that you have given to them will motivate and turn them in the right direction toward their own futures of unending adventures. Give them the knowledge that life has given them unending free gifts found in nature. And, teach them the value of kindness. Give them a strong foundation to begin writing their own stories, starting with the power of faith. And remember, we don't always like our kids, but they are truly blessings, and it is okay to not like them sometimes.

Life is a challenge. Face it and dive into it with zest and energy. Enjoy life and it will give back to you all that you invest into it a hundred times over.

Don't stress about everyday burdens such as housework and tedious daily chores. Do what you feel comfortable doing. Do get things done, but in your own time. Don't procrastinate, but remember your priorities. Priorities are those things that are important to you. **Set priorities.**

You have to organize your daily life so you will have more time for your goals and dreams. Time is more valuable than money, life is time, organize it to your advantage.

You have been exposed to a new theory about life that puts you and your dreams first, while doing the best job you can as a person. You know about faith and the power it can have in your life and you know that you are important, just as important as the next guy, so respect yourself and expect others to respect you as well.

Work slowly toward changing your life into what you want it to be, remember, it is the journey and not the destination. Take small steps, you are moving forward and enjoying your journey.

Everything you do is an experience that you can use, even things that disrupt your life in some way. Know that everything will not always go the way you planned. In life there is always going to be pain and loss, but also there will be fulfilled dreams and goals that have become a reality. Appreciate life; squeeze every drop out of it. Take all you need and want from life and be willing to give something back. Most important, be happy and have faith.

Life is a series of choices. The choices you make will determine the road you will walk. Choices can be changed and new roads can be taken at any time in this life. Choices are the core of our life. Choices remind us that life is fluid and that we have complete control over our lives. If you make a bad choice, change it and move on.

Change your thoughts and change your life. Your thoughts make up who you are. Your thoughts are you.

Life is wonderful, even at its worse. Make your choices and enjoy your life. Write your story and move forward. Take everything life offers you.

This book can be summed up like this: Do what ever you want to do in life, without guilt or fear. Take risks, make choices, and make goals and dreams your priority. Help others. Remember, if you fall down seven times, get up eight. Make a lot of memories, be happy, and count your blessings. Take care of you. You are important. You are blessed. And, you deserve everything life has to offer.

I wish you an abundance of happiness and success as you travel on your journey toward your goals, dreams, and your life story.

THE BEGINNING

If you have any comments, questions, or would like to place an order, I can be contacted at www.srhodesbooks.com